PRAISE FOR /

"Lior Arussy's new book provides a clear road map to one of the biggest challenges of our times – not just dealing with change, but embracing it and thriving in it. Lior's common sense approach provides simple, clear examples of how all of us can stop living in fear of change and develop the resilience needed for the relentless pursuit of What's Next."

Jeff Dailey, CEO of Farmers Insurance

"Lior Arussy definitely succeeds in presenting a novel, refreshing, practice-based perspective on change resilience, which undoubtedly contributes a significant added value to the literature on change in organizations and individuals as well."

Dr. Michael Bar-Eli, Professor and Chair of Business Administration at Ben-Gurion University, and author of *BOOST!*

"The Greek philosopher Heraclitus is credited with saying the 'only constant is change.' Today, effectively embracing that constant is inextricably linked to business survival. *Next Is Now* is a revolutionary, yet pragmatic guide to not only managing change but driving and thriving in a world of cataclysmic explosions of information and technology. Lior Arussy has been entrusted to lead customer-centric change initiatives for some of the world's most iconic brands. His effectiveness, expertise and wisdom jump off the pages of this book. What are you waiting for? Buy *Next Is Now* and thrive when so many others will struggle to position their teams and business for the opportunities ahead."

Joseph Michelli, New York Times #1 bestselling author of books like *Driven to Delight, The New Gold Standard, The Zappos Experience* and *Leading the Starbucks Way*

"Lior Arussy provides a comprehensive and instructive road map for leading change and preparing yourself and your organization for the future. He generously shares insider insights, examples and lessons learned from his many years advising top business leaders."

Denise Lee Yohn, author of *What Great Brands Do* and *FUSION: How Integrating Brand and Culture Powers the World's Greatest Companies*

"One our greatest business challenges is embracing change. In *Next Is Now*, Lior Arussy provides an elegant framework for not only dealing with disruption, but making a fast-changing market landscape your competitive advantage! Read this book to stay one step ahead."

Tim Sanders, New York Times bestselling author of *Love Is the Killer App: How to Win Business and Influence People*

"We live in a very complex, ambiguous and dynamic environment called the 21st century. The ability to embrace change effectively is critical to our success. The five-step process introduced in this book will help you get there. Read this book and learn from one of the best!"

John Maketa, Chief Revenue Officer, Caliper Corp, and co-author of *Now You're Thinking!* and *Leading with Vision*

LIOR ARUSSY

NEXT
IS
NOW

5 STEPS FOR EMBRACING CHANGE

– BUILDING A BUSINESS THAT THRIVES INTO THE FUTURE

LONDON   NEW YORK   SHANGHAI
MADRID   BARCELONA   BOGOTA
MEXICO CITY   MONTERREY   BUENOS AIRES

Published by
LID Publishing Limited
The Record Hall, Studio 204,
16-16a Baldwins Gardens,
London EC1N 7RJ, UK

524 Broadway, 11th Floor, Suite 08-120,
New York, NY 10012, US

info@lidpublishing.com
www.lidpublishing.com

A member of:

BPR
Business Publishers Roundtable

www.businesspublishersroundtable.com

Printed in Great Britain by TJ International
ISBN: 978-1-912555-24-6

Cover design: Caroline Li

CONTENTS

Dedicated with love to Drora,
for turning every change challenge
into an experience and never forgetting our cause.

Don't let what you know limit what you can imagine.
– William C. Taylor

I have spent the past 30 years – first as a young editor at the *Harvard Business Review*, then as cofounder of *Fast Company* magazine, now as an author and lecturer – thinking about, writing about, and otherwise wrestling with the hard work of big change. Every so often (and it is, sadly, all too rare), I meet a thinker, or interact with a consultant, or read a book that has a tremendous impact on how I make sense of the forces of disruption that surround us, and illuminates the challenges for leaders who aim to master those forces and renew their organizations. That's why I stand in awe of Lior Arussy. He is a true 'triple threat' of transformation – as a thinker, consultant and author, his ideas, methodologies and messages amount to a manifesto on the urgency of change and a manifesto for making it happen.

Before I explore the key themes of Lior's important new book and what it means for the future of competition and leadership,

I'd like to pay a quick visit to the past. Back in the mid-nineties, right after we published the first issue of *Fast Company*, we organized a major conference around the question "How Do You Overthrow a Successful Company?" It wasn't a gathering of young Silicon Valley hotshots eager to take on the business establishment (although that was a target audience for the magazine). It was a gathering of strategists, technologists and marketers from organizations that had been around for decades, organizations that were icons in their fields, who sensed that there was turbulence and turmoil all around them – huge shifts in markets, technology and culture – and who were determined to reckon with those shifts and rethink and reimagine every aspect of how they did business and got results. Today, more than two decades later, that question feels more relevant (and vexing) than ever. That's because the work of making deep-seated, meaningful change – building on all your past success, even as you build out a whole new point of view on the future – has become the defining work of our generation. That's the question every leader must seek to answer, that's the work every leader signs up to do – and that's the challenge Lior Arussy faces head-on in *Next Is Now*.

How to set the stage for this urgent, provocative and inexhaustibly useful book? Perhaps the most worthwhile service I can provide is to highlight just a few of the key messages I took away, insights that I believe will be most valuable to everyone who reads it. I will be the first to admit that what strikes me as especially provocative or eye-opening may not strike you in the same way. There is so much unconventional thinking here, so many rich case studies and useful lessons, that every reader may walk away with a slightly different set of personal takeaways.

Here's my first big takeaway: *We are living in a world where ordinary is simply not an option.* Lior's analysis of the forces of change, disruption and innovation are really a plea for originality – among companies, brands and leaders themselves. You can't do big things anymore if you are content with doing things a little better than everyone else or a little differently from how you did them in the past. The goal is no longer to be the best at what lots of other organizations and people already do. It's to be the *only* one who does what you do. What do you promise that only you can promise? What can you deliver that no one else can deliver? What are you prepared to do – for customers, with partners, with your colleagues – that other organizations simply can't or won't do? Those are the questions that help you invent the future – and that this book helps you to answer.

But they are also, truth be told, questions that make most of us quite uncomfortable. Which leads to my second big takeaway: *The more things change, the more the worries and objections to change remain the same.* This book is refreshingly honest about the obstacles – both organizational and individual – that stand between our intellectual recognition of what changes we need to unleash and our psychological and emotional willingness to do what needs doing. But don't take Lior's word for it – listen to a voice from long ago, one more quick visit to the past. If you go back to the very first issue of *Fast Company*, you'll find a thoroughly entertaining article by a fellow named E. F. Borisch.

He was the son of the founder of a very successful manufacturing company in the Midwest, an outfit called the Milwaukee Gear Company, and he was the definition of a change agent. He had all sorts of bold ideas about new markets, customer service, reorganizing the workforce. Yet every time he introduced an idea, he'd get pushback and objections and worries.

So he sat down and wrote an article called "Fifty Reasons Why We Cannot Change," which we happily published. There was no introduction to the article, no conclusion, just a numbered list, from one to fifty, of all the worries and complaints Borisch had heard. What was so funny about the list was that so many of the objections contradicted one another. Reason #1: "We've never done it before." Reason #4: "We already tried it before." Reason #7: "It won't work in a small company." Reason #8: "It won't work in a large company." On and on it went, fifty reasons, each more contradictory than the last.

Now, here's the punch line: We published that article in our first issue, more than 20 years ago. But all we did was reprint an article that E. F. Borisch first published in 1959 – nearly 60 years ago now. Our message to readers back then, and my message to readers of Lior's book now, is that we are in a world where 'playing it safe' may well be the most dangerous course of all. Change begins to happen when leaders convince their colleagues (and themselves) that the risk of trying something new is actually less than the cost of clinging to the status quo.

There are so many more key messages I could highlight, so many takeaways that have shaped how I make sense of the leadership challenges facing all of us, but I am eager for you to dive into the book and find the ideas that resonate most with you. I will, however, conclude by emphasizing what I believe may be Lior's most important insight, and one that far too many of us overlook when we treat business as a largely intellectual or financial exercise. That insight: the hard work of big change is intensely personal. In other words, *you can't unleash deep-seated transformation in your organization unless you are prepared to wrestle with deep-seated transformation of yourself.*

Which is why, I believe, the most effective leaders are the most insatiable learners. Sure, they want to make their organizations and brands more interesting – that's an urgent challenge in this age of disruption. But to do that, they themselves must stay *interested* – in bold new ideas, in small gestures that send big signals, in the enduring mission of their enterprise and all new ways to bring that mission to life. You can't be a great leader, especially in an age of disruption and transformation, unless you are a voracious learner. The central challenge for leaders today is to make sure that all of your expertise – the strategies, practices and assumptions that allowed you to rise through the ranks – don't get in the way of the innovations necessary to create a more compelling future. Put simply, you can't let what you know limit what you can imagine going forward.

Next Is Now is a powerful tool to help you rethink and reimagine what's possible, to start learning as fast as the world is changing. I would urge you not just to read it, but to highlight it, to wrestle with it, to figure out ways, large and small, to put it to work in your organization and for your career. This book will make sure that what you know doesn't limit what you can imagine.

Bill Taylor is the cofounder of *Fast Company* magazine and the author, most recently, of *Simply Brilliant: How Great Organizations Do Ordinary Things in Extraordinary Ways.*

THE NEXT IS NOW

This is not a book about change. It is a book about THE change. The change you live through every day. The change that doesn't go away. The one you are still in denial about. This book is the wake-up call to own the change before it owns you.

The magnitude of change around us is so sweeping, we fail to see the forest for the trees. Change is no longer a few new trees in a familiar forest. It is an entirely new forest. And then a new one every day for the rest of our lives. Are you ready for it? This book is about not fearing that new forest of change, and owning it with pleasure and delight. Finding meaning in the big change and shaping it to become full of purpose. If you are ready to embrace change as a life and business accelerator, let's get going.

In 1888, Bertha Benz, wife of Mercedes-Benz founder Karl Benz, drove one of his cars more than 60 miles to visit her parents.

She didn't bother to inform her husband that she was about to embark on the longest drive ever attempted. The trip wasn't just an impressive feat for a feisty 19th century woman; it was a true technological milestone – it marked the point when cars became a mainstream mode of transportation.

Fast-forward 125 years to 2013 – the year when another Mercedes covered the same route.

This time, without a driver.

There are still plenty of technological and regulatory hurdles to jump before driverless cars become the norm, but imagine for a moment the impact they will have on the automobile, delivery and transportation industries – to name just a few. This technology will transform not only the way we drive, but the way we build roads and design cities.

Ultimately it will offer a new way to live and be mobile. Are you ready for this change? Eager for its arrival? Or reluctant to see it coming?

But this change is not isolated. If you are among the people working in architecture, construction, and transportation, you are hardly the only one in danger of having your role usurped by new technologies. A wide range of industries – from hospitality and retail to education, music and healthcare – are undergoing radical transformations thanks to technological innovation, evolving customer tastes and new business models such as the on-demand economy. These changes are not simply passing trends. They are the new reality.

Change is no longer the exception, it's the rule. And it is going to rule you, unless you take charge.

In other words, the Next Is Now.

As you think of change, here is a question to contemplate: How much change are you resisting at the moment? At work? In life? With your health?

How much time and effort are you spending on fighting change instead of evaluating its merits? Are you even aware of the natural resistance you have toward change?

We usually fight change in many different ways: acting with reluctance, fighting it head-on, running away from it, denying it, ignoring it and behaving in a passive-aggressive way toward it. Our natural state seems to be fight-or-flight, but not to embrace it. You must admit this is exhausting, and we usually lose the fight, arriving at the finish line late and defeated. But even in the few cases where we manage to muster a victory over change, it is a lame one. Because the victory means we lost relevance. We stay behind. There must be a better way. We must stop fighting change just for the sake of resisting. We need a new way to embrace the Next and enjoy it. Is it possible to enjoy it? Welcome to the journey.

◆ ◆ ◆

Adapting to change is absolutely critical to survival in both business and in life, yet countless studies tell us how difficult it is for individuals and organizations to change. Why?

Change creates an identity crisis. Most of us can't help but feel that 'the new way of doing things' we're being sold is a response to some failure on our part. Otherwise, why change? And so, while a new approach or habit may make rational sense, it can simultaneously threaten our self-esteem, our sense of financial security and our belief systems.

How many of us have spent years mastering a technique or technology only to be informed about some hot new system – and the cool young team being brought in to train us? Will we be able to keep up? Or is it just a matter of time before our company trades us in for younger, cheaper hires? How many of us have stayed in a job we hated just because the leap into the unknown was too overwhelming? Ignored our doctor's advice because old habits were too hard to break? (If you're not raising your hand, perhaps you're in more denial about your resistance to change than I imagined!)

All the data and so-called rational arguments won't penetrate the emotional wall of rejection and fear of change that we all possess. What's worse: even if you are ready to embrace change, those who work with you may not be ready to support your efforts; all it takes is a few people dragging their heels, and the millions of dollars you've spent on change-management techniques will be wasted.

For decades, leading thinkers from the world of psychology and management have tackled the tricky subject of change. But have these ideas led to any successful change initiatives? To discover the answer to that question, the consultancy I founded, Strativity, conducted a survey with the *Harvard Business Review* to understand the state of change execution. The study benchmarked 422 organizations and their current state of implementing change programs. The results were shocking.

We learned that organizational change efforts succeed a mere 9% of the time. Yes, you read that right: *fewer than one in ten transformation attempts succeed,* despite all of the well-meaning – but wholly theoretical – advice in books on change. If Strativity delivered results like that, we wouldn't have made it through our first year.

Clearly, we need a new approach.

For the past 15 years, my colleagues and I have helped companies drive deep, profound change initiatives that support both the customer journey and our clients' profitability. After leading more than 200 successful change efforts at Fortune 500 companies, one thing has become very clear to us: we must change the way we change. Broad, sweeping statements are not going to cut it. Top-down directives will not drive the desired transformation.

And it's not just executives who need this wake-up call. I've written this book for every person grappling with change, not just those leading change initiatives. (Hint: that means all of us.) Whether you're a front-line worker or a freelancer, the ability to reinvent yourself – and fast – is probably the most important skill you will need in the future. We cannot predict what the future will bring, but there is plenty of compelling evidence that those who embrace change will reap the rewards of financial stability and marketplace relevance.

While the decision to drive change may fall to a company's leaders or the clients sending us our 1099s, change itself takes place within each one of us. In other words, it's not your manager's or your customer's job to inspire you to change. It's your responsibility to learn what is arguably the most crucial 21st century skill: adaptability.

Are You Open to Change?

Imagine, for a moment, your favourite band. You know the one. The one you always count on to help you celebrate the highs and lift you out of the lows. When did you discover them? How old were you?

Let me guess. You were probably in your teens – maybe your twenties. If you're over 33, you probably have some very strong opinions about 'what the kids are listening to today'. If this sounds anything like you, you're not alone. A Spotify Insights and Echo Nest study discovered that most people's musical tastes evolve until the age of 25 and mature at the age of 35.

After that they get ... stuck. People cling to their old music and dismiss anything new.

Not long ago, a number of managers complained to me that they can't understand the millennial employees joining their ranks. I asked them about their favourite music; not surprisingly, their lists included mostly bands they had grown up with.

"You're not open enough to listen to their music," I said. "How could you ever understand them?"

We all think we are open to change, but the facts show us otherwise. In this book I will explore the reasons why we resist change, help you diagnose your own approach to change and reveal a proven methodology for strengthening what we refer to as your 'change resilience' – in other words, how quickly and meaningfully you or your organization implements change.

Stuck in a rut? Try a new technology. Go to the millennial sitting next to you and check out what tools that person uses. How does she create presentations? And then go and learn those tools. Stretch yourself out of your comfort zone and start owning new tools for your success.

Change Isn't an Event

Quick. Without thinking too hard, consider how you or the companies you've worked for have approached change in the past.

If you're like many of the individuals and companies we've worked with, you probably kicked things off with some planning, penciled in a day to launch your Big New Thing/Habit/Life, and ... after your excitement died down a couple weeks (or even days) later, returned to some modified version of normalcy. If you're really honest with yourself, you're not seeing anywhere near the results you'd hoped for.

Why? Because you treated change as an *event* – often an unpleasant one – that you needed to get through.

Take a moment to think about how you treat unpleasant events – for example, a root canal or your taxes. You probably put it off for as long as you can. You postpone it. You think: *I can wait.* But change isn't an event. It's not something you can postpone, because it's already here – and waiting to address it has a price.

Return on Nothing

One of our clients learned the price of ignoring change after they called us in to help them analyse whether to purchase new customer-relationship software. The software promised to stream-line the process of ordering and managing inventory to ensure reorders and renewals, but, as I'm sure you can imagine, the company's sales team already had their own methods for connecting with customers – the last thing they wanted was to change things up. Plus the software was expensive and required training that would affect the client's quarterly targets.

"Hey, we're still making our numbers," my client told me. "Be-sides, our main competitor isn't even using this software yet. We'll get to it when we get to it."

"Actually, your competition is not the other guys," I said upon hearing this. "You're both losing to a third competitor: doing nothing."

We created a calculator called Return on Nothing that mea-sured sales lost to doing things the old decentralized, ad hoc way. We discovered that our client was losing potential customers at a rate of about 19% a year because they had no streamlined process for renewing orders or introducing new solutions. Our client thought doing nothing was saving them money. But in reality they were losing significant market share.

Change Schedules Itself

You can't just schedule change into your Outlook at your convenience. It schedules itself, whether you like it or not. Sure, we can keep postponing our response to change. But there is a cost. Unless we understand that and manage change accordingly, we can anticipate a lot of unrealized expectations. Unfortunately, most of us manage change poorly – if we try to manage it at all.

More often than not, the signs that change is coming are as clear as day – and yet we pull down the shades. Is there any better example than the parents who drop their kid off at his freshman dorm and then are struck with the sudden realization that the nest is empty?

With five kids of my own, I can certainly sympathize, but you can't tell me you didn't know this was coming. This is one change you had 18 years to plan for! You've had two decades to prepare, and you're still acting like, "Oh my gosh, what just happened?"

Of course, it's a natural human reaction to push dealing with change off for as long as possible. That's why the Future Ready Impact methodology starts by taking stock of where a company is when it comes to major change endeavours. Whenever our teams start working with a new client, we frequently find a lot of works-in-progress and not a lot of success stories. One of our clients had *more than 30 change programs* they were attempting to launch in less than four years!

But before we judge them too harshly, keep in mind that they're hardly the only ones to demonstrate this lack of focus around change. Who among us doesn't have a laundry list of things we'd like to change about our careers and our lives? I'll wager that you've made a lot of resolutions over the years, yet only stuck to a handful of them, telling yourself, *Tomorrow, I swear...*

The challenge is: when it comes to the kind of economic changes we're all facing today, we can't keep pushing off change. And we certainly no longer have the luxury of planning for change three, four, five years out. We have to tackle new challenges head-on as they arise.

This is what it means to be future ready.

Great Starts, Glorious Failures

When the *Harvard Business Review*, in conjunction with Strativity, conducted our landmark study on change, we sought answers to several questions.

1. How much change are organizations facing today?

2. How do they justify change programs?

3. How are they doing in terms of implementing change?

4. If they're not having success, why?

5. How must they adapt to increase their success rate?

Thanks to the responses of 422 executives from companies of all sizes and a number of industries, we discovered that people are having even more difficulty than we imagined. An astonishing 86% of the respondents confirmed what we suspected: they are attempting to execute multiple change initiatives simultaneously. Different business functions – from operations and IT to marketing and finance – are trying to tackle different issues concurrently.

But this only increases the pressure on the organization. When it comes to justifying each program and allocating resources, every department can naturally point to its own very clear return on investment or productivity gain targets. And yet, 91% of those same respondents have experienced a change initiative failure in their organization. That's nearly all of them! Apparently there's a disconnect between our expectations around change and the reality.

The reasons change programs fail vary, but one theme seems to stand out. It may surprise you to learn that when participants in our survey were asked to create a list of reasons for failure, 'insufficient budget' was cited by 23% and 'insufficient time' by only 17%. Instead, participants ranked the following issues as the most critical:

+ Poor communication: 62%

+ Insufficient leadership sponsorship and
  support: 54%

+ Organizational politics: 50%

+ Lack of understanding of the purpose of
  the change: 50%

+ Lack of user buy-in: 42%

+ Lack of collaboration: 40%

What do all of these issues have in common?

They are all *human* problems. Even when a strong case has been made that a change will have a positive financial impact, people aren't changing. When I talk about people, I mean you and me. It's we who are fighting it in various ways, ranging from fake embrace to completely ignoring it. We muster our creativity to stop the unstoppable and avoid the unavoidable.

As leadership, we are not driving the change; and as employees, we are not buying in. In other words, people (again, you and me) at even the most disciplined organizations are acting emotionally, not logically. And since the majority of problems are neither time- nor budget-related, changing the deadline or allocating more resources will do nothing to address the real challenge.

The study also illustrates that a large capability gap is causing widespread failure in change initiatives. With poor communication as an obstacle 62% of the time and a lack of understanding about the purpose of a change program derailing 50% of initiatives, it seems as though organizations are either ignoring the human factor or taking it for granted.

Either way, they are not anything close to future ready.

The Sum Total of Personal Choices

Who makes the decision about whether a personal or organizational transformation will take root?

Contrary to popular perception, change is not decided at the top. It's not something we'll do just because someone in a position of authority tells us to. Accepting change is a personal choice: each person must decide whether they're on board with a change and how far they will take its implementation. Sure, top executives can mandate usage of a new technology or adopt new metrics that will force employees to act in one way and not another – but such changes are superficial and will be implemented reluctantly. Our therapists, spiritual mentors and financial coaches can give us all the clever advice in the world, but that doesn't mean we're going to do what they say.

One of the most common pitfalls of change efforts occurs when companies devote most of their resources to gaining executive-level buy-in, but do very little to engage employees early on in the change process. It is puzzling to see companies spending $50 million on a new technology platform but less than $100,000 on employee engagement. The assumption is that employees will blindly follow whatever top management decides. Employees are treated as passive followers who will do whatever they are being told to do.

The reality could not be more different. An organization is not simply the outcome of executives' decisions – it is the sum total of its employees' choices. Remember, in a lot of companies, the customer will never see the CEO or meet the VP of sales.

Customers are solely in the hands of the front-line employees. If those employees do not make the choice to live the change every day, then no strategy will be executed.

But it's not just companies that make this mistake. How many of us are quick to blow a ton of money on self-help programs, transformational workshops or expensive trainers, hoping for some expert to tell us exactly how to change our lives – but as soon as we realize that changing our lives requires us to actually *change our behaviour*, we want a refund.

When we've discussed this simple truth – that change is deeply personal – with leadership at organizations, many executives refuse to accept it. Most don't want to hear that they are at the mercy of their employees. After all, they worked hard to get to where they are. They shoulder more financial responsibility than their employees and have to make choices that can have a deeper impact on the organization – why wouldn't employees trust them when they say a change needs to be made?

Then there are enlightened executives who agree that employees determine the future success of strategy and change – until it comes time to talk about budget. They fail to find room in the budget for training and empowering employees at every level of the organization. Or they argue that there is not enough time to engage all employees in this process. My answer to that is simple: think again, and do it fast. There is no alternative to engaging employees in a meaningful way as soon as possible. The sooner they get engaged and embrace it, the faster your change initiative will be implemented and the better the outcome it will deliver.

Whatever time or money you think you will save on the front end by not engaging employees, you will waste on the back end with useless delays, political battles and reduced impact.

If you are the person being asked to change, you most likely feel like a victim. Maybe the change is being dictated from above – you've been given a tight deadline and little to no context. Your CEO has announced 'the new direction' or 'the way of the future' on a wide screen with complex diagrams. And you stare at all this and try to figure out: *Seriously? What is really going on here? What was wrong with the way we were doing things before? Why do we need to change, and how will this impact my plans to take the kids on a vacation to Hawaii? I am overworked as it is – and now this. It's the last thing I need.*

Or is it?

While it's easy to play the role of passive victim, most changes are presented to us for a reason. And unless you think your CEO is trying to run your organization into the ground, your coach is trying to sabotage your career or your doctor wants you to stay sick, there is a high likelihood that this change has an upside for everyone – including you. Most likely a proposed change is a response to circumstances beyond your control.

When there's a storm on the horizon that requires you to steer the ship north, believe me, you don't want to be paddling east. It doesn't matter how impressive your previous voyages have been; you have to deal with what's happening *now*. This book is designed to help you embrace and even help accelerate change, develop change resilience and be more relevant to the future of your industry or organization.

Change with an Impact

In the pages that follow, I will share a five-step Future Ready Impact methodology that can guide anyone, regardless of their industry or role, through the process of taking ownership over change. By focusing on intrinsically motivating people at every layer of our clients' organizations, our process has helped a number of leading companies improve in ways they never imagined possible.

I wrote this book to share our unique approach to change with anyone committed to ongoing transformation. While most of my experience is drawn from working with organizations, organizations are the sum total of people and their fears, hopes and aspirations. We take a human-centric approach to developing change resilience that will be equally applicable to your personal life – whether you're learning to care for a newborn, grappling with a strong-willed teenager, handling an unexpected medical condition, or even winning the lottery. Life is full of unexpected turns and tribulations. We can't control those changes, but we can control our response to them. By cultivating change resilience, we can empower ourselves to thrive amid even the most life-altering events.

Change Is Personal

My curiosity about how human beings deal with the constantly evolving nature of life preceded the launch of my consultancy. Perhaps it's because I've experienced so many changes in my own life

– personal, professional, you name it. In fact, at times it can seem as if the one constant in my life is change!

I grew up in a neighborhood outside Tel Aviv, Israel, where we valued family and friendship above all. Visiting your friends didn't require planning a playdate four weeks in advance. You simply showed up and knocked on the door. There was camaraderie among us that you will not find in the many places where individuality reigns supreme. We consider family – not the individual – the smallest organizational unit, so we were taught to do whatever it takes to help and protect the family.

When I left home and moved to the US, I encountered a brave new world full of optimism about the power of the individual to change the world – and I experienced a true culture shock. This worldview was enticing and inspiring but, as I later discovered, it came with a price. Where I came from, we all wanted to succeed and have better lives. But we never saw this as something that would come at the expense of friendship and our joint celebrations. The obsession with individual achievements and grades and the ruthless competition for college acceptance was as foreign to me as speaking in ancient Mandarin.

Since my first move, I have lived in many cities, including Tel Aviv (again); Cleveland; Milan; London; Sunnyvale, California; and Livingston, New Jersey. Each move challenged me to find my way in a new setting – I had to adapt both culturally and geographically (as well as gastronomically).

That was hardly the only personal change I've experienced. When my first daughter was born, I felt empowered and ready.

But as any parent will tell you, all the preparation in the world won't prepare you for the act of actual parenting. By the time my next daughter was born, I felt knowledgeable – but so many parenting techniques that worked with our first child fell disappointingly short. When my third daughter arrived, I was sure I had nailed this parenting thing. Boy, was I wrong.

Today I'm raising five children with my loving wife. But each child is different and requires a different parental and communication style. Many times, I need to switch back and forth between these styles in less than a second. One of my daughters is the ultimate introvert, speaking only when she has something meaningful to say. Another daughter speaks as a matter of thinking. Imagine sitting for dinner with both!

I've experienced a fair amount of professional changes as well. I started my career in technology sales and marketing for both start-ups and multinational corporations, including Hewlett-Packard. When, in 2003, I decided to switch my career to consulting, I didn't know the first thing about it. I knew shifting careers would require some reinvention, but I had no idea how much change I would experience. I didn't even know how to price my services – yes, some of my first clients got a bargain, but I love them for trusting me in the early days. So we both benefited from the arrangement.

Fifteen years later, I have used my fascination with change resilience to build a consultancy dedicated to helping companies embrace change from the ground up. Even after all this time, I am still amazed at how nimble I have to be when it comes to understanding the unique culture of each company. I remember when one client told me the secret to success at his firm: "Always walk fast and look worried." It was, needless to say, a strange culture to be part of.

On any given day, I may start off with a discussion about the future of healthcare, shift into a talk about luxury vehicles, discuss the latest digital trends in hospitality and close the day with a tough discussion about how to motivate cynical employees at a utility company. My business requires me to travel around 200,000 miles a year. I travel so much I often forget which city I am in. Change happens all the time in my line of work – and it happens fast.

My company is still growing – and growing pains are par for the course. While I'm proud that Strativity has three times been named to *Consulting Magazine*'s list of fastest-growing firms, as well as selected as one of the magazine's Seven Small Jewels, an award bestowed upon the most promising boutique consulting firms, the amount of change that occurs during periods of growth is daunting.

When you've had to adapt as much as I have, you start to see intense change as a way of life – and even as a way to build a bridge between worlds. Change means coming up with new ways to balance my family and my work, finding home in places far from where I came from. As a result, I believe change is deeply personal.

How do I handle it?

Let me tell you a story that I believe will illustrate how.

I've noticed that when one of my employees is criticized by a client or partner, I often jump to defend them in ways that they didn't expect. Not long ago, a manager who'd joined our team from one of the Big Four consulting firms expressed shock when I defended the actions of a junior consultant and asked the client to apologize. He told me that his previous employer would have thrown that junior consultant under the bus and replaced him without argument.

It's moments like this when my core values surface. I have never forgotten the important role that family has always played in my life, and I treat my friends and employees accordingly. This value is what guides me through periods of massive change. I use it as a kind of compass. I ask myself: *How will the change help me better serve the people I care about?*

Once I have the answer to that question, my next steps are a lot clearer.

Your values, too, can guide you through the difficult but necessary changes you'll face in your life and career. That's why a key part of our methodology involves focusing on what will never change: your commitment to doing your job well, delivering a great experience to your customers, and taking care of yourself and your loved ones.

A quick note: I use the word *customers* to refer to everyone whose lives will be affected by the new change we're considering. In many instances, this may mean your company's literal customers – or it might mean the internal customers whom you serve. But while our methodology is one that's most frequently embraced in a business context, we've found that it's equally effective when grappling with change in our personal lives. It doesn't matter whether the change you're dealing with is a new IT system your manager has asked you to use or your bank's new investment app: the tools you can use to face your fears and weather the uncertainty ahead are the same.

This methodology is all about focusing on what's most important: the positive impact we can make in the lives of others by becoming more change resilient. It's not about ditching your values – quite the contrary. It's about connecting to them on an even deeper level.

So if you're worried about the change ahead, you can take a deep breath. The work you're about to do is all about finding a firm foundation so that you can approach change from a place of strength and flexibility.

How to Use This Book

It's a lot easier to achieve our goals when we have someone holding us accountable. A trainer, a coach – you know, the person who's tough on you but doesn't give up on you. The person who doesn't let you cut any corners. The one who challenges you to go further than you think you can.

When it comes to embracing change, we need such a trainer. We need someone who won't allow us to romanticize the past. Someone to remind us that the future is already happening. Someone who makes us stick to our New Year's resolutions.

Don't worry, that's me.

But what's a trainer without a program?

At the heart of this book is a program that will provide you with the insights, inspiration and tools to embrace the ever-changing world we live in. You will learn to adapt to the times without forgetting the past or losing your connection to your core values. You will learn to view change not as an identity crisis but rather as the natural evolution of the person you already are.

This book is divided into three parts. In the first, we'll explore the reasons why change can seem like such an existential threat. You'll identify your own 'change personality' – which will give you a better grasp of how to overcome any resistance to change you might have. For managers, insight into the different change personalities will give you an edge when it comes to getting your teams on board with new systems and strategies.

In the second part of the book, I'll lay out a five-step methodology for becoming future ready that is equally applicable when approaching changes at work and in your personal life. And in the third, I'll share techniques designed to help you live with change and use your increased change resilience to lead others.

If you are resolved to embrace change and face it from a place of strength, this is your book. If you recognize that change is happening faster than ever and you need a companion on the journey, you're in the right place.

PART ONE

one

CHANGE RESILIENCE

Connecting to Your Core Cause

Up until very recently, doctors enjoyed an undeniable prestige. After completing many years of medical school, they came to possess special skills. They were considered the healers of the human race. Their decisions were final, and patients accepted their instructions without a challenge.

Today, it is common practice for patients to show up with data collected from unknown sources on the internet and challenge their physicians' recommendations. Doctors find themselves justifying their advice to patients who may not have taken even a single college course, let alone have professional medical expertise. In the name of "It's my body" and "I found it on the internet," patients are redefining the medical profession in ways we are still trying to fully understand.

Thanks to patient empowerment and immediate access to medical insight on the internet, veteran physicians feel threatened.

Every new resident in their hospitals can now tap into knowledge that took them years to accumulate through hard work and trial and error. The entire medical profession is going through a seismic change we have yet to see the full impact of.

And it's not the only one.

Entire industries are disappearing and undergoing fundamental changes at a pace we have never encountered before. The music business was altered forever with the creation of iTunes and streaming services. The automobile industry is starting to feel the pinch from ride-sharing companies like Zipcar. Banking is now done online with a slew of new financial empowerment tools that turn every millennial into an educated banker. Travel agents? A distant, fading memory.

Our natural reaction to all of this change is resistance. And the more change thrown at us, the greater our resistance. If we are not future ready, we reject it. But the price of our aversion to change is a loss of marketplace relevance. It hinders our ability to continue to make an impact on a world that's evolving faster than ever before.

When I work with companies and individuals looking to develop change resilience, I ask them to recognize the emotional aspect of change. If employees are emotionally ready for change, the chance that a new strategy will succeed is exponentially higher. After all, the human body can only handle so much change – and the same is true of an organization made up of large groups of human beings. So whether you're leading a change at your organization or being asked to take part in one, take heart: in this approach, we start by remembering everything that doesn't change.

We do this by identifying our 'core cause' – in other words, our individual or organizational responsibilities, our mission, our values. Your core cause is a bridge that stretches from your past or your company's earliest days into the future. While change may seem a step out into the unknown, if your connection to your core cause is strong enough, you'll be supported the whole way.

Redefining Authority

I love art and have always found paintings and sculptures fascinating. And I admire the artists who create them. But when it came to Joan Miró, I got stuck. No matter what, I failed to see the greatness expressed in dots and lines drawn on a white canvas. I once spent four hours listening to an audio guide while walking about the Miró museum in Barcelona. It didn't help. I still failed to understand it. And I felt stupid about it, for he is one of the greats – the whole world finds him a genius, paying millions of dollars for his original masterpieces. I am confident you have your own examples of artists or even a period of art you simply fail to understand, and maybe you too feel foolish for it. After all, the authorities say he is great, so there must be something wrong with *you*.

In a world of external authorities telling us what is good and what is bad, defining what is beautiful and what should be ignored, what is a significant work of art and what is rubbish, we often feel passive and insignificant. However, the seismic changes we are experiencing not just with our physicians but with our clergymen, financial advisors, professors, artists, managers, salespeople, interior designers, parents and any other force of expertise, are amounting to nothing short of redefining authorities.

In some cases, traditional centralized authorities have disappointed many people with self-serving agendas that erode trust to a point that we simply ignore them or consider their opinion with a healthy dose of suspicion.

We've rebelled against traditional centralized authority and have taken the reign of authority away from them. We can do it just as well as they do it. We have the research tools and a network of friends who can advise us. And when we need to, we will consult with the old guard of centralized authority, but we will make our own decisions.

A confluence of several forces brought upon the redefinition of authority. When combining the transparency and abundance of knowledge with the growth of peer-to-peer sharing and the loss of trust in traditional experts, we experience the rise of a new class of experts: us. We are the new authorities.

Authority has been decentralized.

It is distributed to all and any who want to assume it.

It is internal to us.

In the new world of us as the authority, there is a new path to knowledge. We now experience it ourselves and form our own opinions. We use products and services as tools, not as a final destination. They enlighten us and provide us with data points to consider. Our personal experience is the ultimate judge.

But. And there is a big BUT attached to this new class of authority. Authority comes with responsibility.

As the source of authority, we ought to assume the accountability of our decisions and own the learning process. We can no longer be passive recipients of others' ideas and decisions.

We, the decision makers, must make the best decisions.

We can no longer afford to sulk about and resist change.

We can no longer play the victim of change.

As the new authorities, we are the change and we must drive it.

The responsibility is now solely on our shoulders.

The new authority ought to proactively drive change.

And when it comes to Miró's work, I will simply accept that it is absolutely okay for me not to get it. And most of all, as a new authority, I will feel great about that.

The Secret Ingredient of Change Resilience

Why do we do the things we do?

There are two possible reasons: either we want to or we have to. Some of our actions are driven by external rewards such as salaries, bonuses and other incentives. Many people work because they have to – not because they want to – and their salary provides ample motivation to do whatever their boss wants them to do. But as soon as they win the lottery, they're out the door.

When we're intrinsically motivated, on the other hand, we do things we believe are right. We take action based on our internal compasses or value systems: we volunteer, create art, adopt a rescue animal, for instance.

External motivation makes us do things we don't want to do.

Intrinsic motivation makes us do things we do want to do – and are proud to.

When we look in the mirror, we love the version of us who operates based on an intrinsic motivation. We often loathe the part of ourselves that is extrinsically motivated. Much has been written about the different kinds of motivation (Daniel Pink's book *Drive* brought the topic well-deserved attention a few years ago), but here's what's most relevant when it comes to embracing the Next: when we introduce the concept of change resilience to people, most mistakenly believe it all boils down to speed. That's part of it, but people also need to believe that change will *make a difference*.

For that reason, an intrinsically motivated person will have a far better chance of developing strong change resilience. That person's pride in making an impact will be a crucial component of his or her ability to adapt to change faster.

The problem is, most organizations are not set up this way. Making room for intrinsic motivation creates a major challenge for organizations because it requires cocreation and what I call 'choice-based decisions,' when the traditional organization focuses on mandates and adherence. Most companies have top-down cultures where employees are treated not as independent decision makers but as 'process operators'. They might help to execute a strategy – but they don't own it.

Unfortunately, this kind of top-down structure can be a huge hindrance to companies looking to stay relevant. Leaders need people to be flexible, take ownership. But it's very difficult to take ownership of something that somebody else did for you.

That's why we've designed a process that makes each and every individual part of the decision process. Even so, whenever we go into a new company, people tell us: "Oh, the decision to change was made from the top." Our choice-based environment can seem disingenuous.

I've observed the demeanor of countless people who think change is being forced upon them. Feeling powerless, they become very passive. They internalize the message: "You don't want my brain, you just want my hands." When I begin work with a new company, they rarely believe that they have a choice. They feel that they're being forced into something – that decisions are being served to them.

In fact, we do give them a choice: a) I provide them with the data points to (I hope) reach the same conclusions as their leaders, and b) I give them the choice to say, "You know what? I'm not staying on board." We remind people that *no* is a choice. It is absolutely a choice.

By giving each person the opportunity to make choices based on data, we create an environment where every person is treated with respect. And we've seen an excellent success rate as a result. When we're not truly committed to a change, we will search for shortcuts, complain to anyone who will listen and make it very clear we don't believe that we're capable of transforming ourselves or our companies. We'll drag our heels, put things off until tomorrow, wait until it seems safer to make a leap. This kind of behaviour is the enemy of impact.

Defining Your Core Cause

Your core cause is the reason you exist. The higher purpose that drives you. It is usually defined by the people you serve or who are enjoying the benefit of your efforts: How do your customers use your product or services? What does it empower or inspire them to do? How does it make their lives better or easier? How do you treat your customers and colleagues? How do you solve their problems?

A core cause should not be confused with the tools or processes you use to help others achieve their goals. Your tools can always change and improve. Your core cause will remain constant.

* For teachers, a core cause might be to educate and inspire, not the tests and quizzes they give.

* For police officers, it is the creation of a sense of safety and security, not the number of arrests they've made.

* For bankers, it is the creation of financial confidence among their clients, not the spreadsheets or formulas they use.

* For healthcare providers, it is the sense of hope in the eyes of a patient, not the injection or stethoscope used in the treatment.

Unfortunately, many people associate their work with the tools they use and not the reason they are using those tools. They get buried in the weeds of their day-to-day jobs and fail to see the impact they're having on customers.

Even if your work does not allow you to see or speak to them regularly, you do have customers. What's more, anyone who lives with the consequences of your actions is someone you have the opportunity to serve and help. That includes your colleagues – your boss, those who report to you, the finance manager who needs to decipher your expense sheet – as well as all the people you come into contact with on a daily basis.

The quality of your work, your attitude and your behaviour have a direct impact on their lives and happiness. You can either take a passive approach, blaming tools and processes for poor outcomes. Or you can take a proactive approach: use the tools you've been given in service of your core cause. Ask yourself:

+ Will I let new processes, tools and systems control me?

+ Or will I take an active role in using them to help others?

When you feel deeply connected to your core cause, specific tools and processes lose their power over you. As a banker who accepts deposits and dispenses cash, you would feel threatened by new banking apps. But as a banker committed to helping people fulfil their dreams, you will see how the evolution of your tools helps you do your job well. After all, the tools you've been using seemingly forever were new once. Once you would have used an abacus, then a calculator, then a computer. Just because it's time to add mobile apps into the mix doesn't mean the banker's role has changed.

The tools will always evolve.

The core cause will not.

The Change-Prevention Program

You know those people who, no matter what you initiate, will always find a way to kill new ideas? We call them the 'change-prevention program' people. (They are the cousins of the 'sales-prevention program' people who create obstacles to success for salespeople.) They are out there and they cost us our future. In a world of big, constant changes, we can no longer tolerate their behaviour and the consequences of their negative, delaying actions. We simply cannot allow them to control the future of the organization and ourselves.

Each time David sent an email or used Microsoft Word, he was playing a small but vital part in an all-out corporate rebellion – and he wasn't alone. Together, he and his colleagues in the customer service department of a $13 billion global industrial manufacturing company were waging war against the executives who were trying to foist a new ordering system upon them without their input.

Now, there was good reason for the proposed change. The industrial products sold by the company were patented – so if something broke, customers would need a replacement right away or a huge piece of machinery would sit dormant for days. In some instances, a customer might lose $2 million because David's company failed to deliver a $50 widget in time.

After receiving multiple customer complaints, the company's leaders realized they needed a new integrated software system. But here's where they made a crucial mistake – management selected and installed the software without first consulting their employees. A company was hired to guide implementation of the new tool, and training was delivered with a very clear attitude: "Shape up or ship out."

But David and his colleagues were not planning to go down quietly. They rebelled. They threatened to miss their targets on purpose if they were forced to use the new system. Ultimately, executive leadership was forced to decide between their sales goals and the new software. The decision they made was a no-brainer: they relented. The new software became optional – which meant that almost no employee used it, and millions of dollars and the promise of a better, more modern way of serving customers were lost.

When my team and I started working with the company, they were embarking on an even bigger change – this time, they were implementing an enterprise management system (SAP) to automate operations, track customers' orders and invoice customers automatically upon shipment of their products. By then, the employees were ready for the fight. They knew what was coming and were prepared to resist until the bitter end. And they were optimistic about their win. After all, the score thus far was in their favour – Change: 0; Employees: 1. And they were energized to repeat their success.

We clearly needed to try something different.

We first asked each employee to think about the impact of the new system. We developed a process that helped them realize on their own that this tool would be important for the future of the company. But we didn't stop there.

We dug deeper and realized that employees were resisting the new technology because they were attached to, and very proud of, the Word and Excel templates they had developed over the years to assist them in their work. They saw themselves and their success through the lens of those tools. It was as if they were losing a limb – a clear threat to their ability to succeed in the future.

Once he learned more about the new software, however, David had an epiphany. He realized that he is not measured by the tools he uses but rather by the impact he makes on his customers. The true measure of success was his ability to move customers emotionally and to develop good relationships with them. And there were many ways for David to achieve that goal.

David also discovered that his old ways were exactly that: old. Customers, to David's shock, perceived his work as dated and irrelevant – and some were seriously considering switching to a competitor who provided a more modern service. In fact, customers were concerned that the old tools represented a deeper issue: the company and its products were out of touch.

We called this discovery "the conversation you never had with your customers, but should have."

CHANGE RESILIENCE CHALLENGE #2

What conversation should you be having with your customers but aren't yet? How can you start the uncomfortable process of adapting before customers demand change?

One of David's biggest discoveries was that his main purpose – delighting customers – would not change. The tools he used to get there were simply evolving. By focusing on what remained consistent between the past and the future, David was more willing not only to embrace change but also to accelerate its adoption. All of a sudden, the new SAP program was not a weight, but a wing. It wasn't a threat, but rather a promise: a new way to grow and nurture his relationships with customers.

Bringing change resilience into David's company was not just about shifting mindsets around a new system. We also needed to modernize the entire process of conducting business – and it wasn't just David's team who had to step up. Another thorny issue was the fax machine – and this time it was the executive team resisting the change. Heeding the advice from one of the Big Four auditing firms, company policy required that every single order be submitted via fax.

It was common knowledge that late delivery of a replacement part would cost clients millions. Yet despite the urgency, David was instructed to tell all inquiring customers that they should hang up the phone and submit their orders by fax. Placing an order via credit card was practically science fiction.

David challenged me personally: "If you can get the CFO to stop this requirement, we're all-in."

The truth was, stock trading was already conducted entirely via phone – there was no reason to use such an archaic system. The faxing rule was an absurd requirement masked in the guise of adherence to financial regulation. The customer service team proposed that they be empowered to take orders over the phone and, as a result, better satisfy their customers.

It was the tipping point. David and his team celebrated the death of the fax process – it was a symbol that change was not a one-way street where all the burden was placed on employees, but rather a mutual commitment to update processes in order to better delight customers. As a result, employees opened up to change. They finally felt that their goals and management's were aligned.

The results we saw just 12 months later exceeded our expectations. Employee morale and commitment were high. Customer satisfaction went up by 20%, and the company soon won a multi-billion-dollar, multiyear contract – their largest contract ever – with one of their customers. The customer cited the recent change program and a customer-centric approach as the primary reasons for the win. The transformation was awarded several prestigious awards and set the company up well when it came to handling new changes and opportunities.

But, as with every transformation, it's not just numbers that reveal success. You can also hear it in the stories that employees tell about their empowerment. Not long after we'd begun working with the company, a call came in to David's customer service centre from Guadalajara, Mexico. The client decided to send a representative to the company's headquarters to buy the needed part and bring it back – in fact, he was already on a plane.

There were so many aspects to this request that were problematic. First, David's office didn't have the part on hand – it was stored in a faraway warehouse. To make matters worse, the customer was not set up in their system, because in Mexico the company's parts were sold exclusively by a distributor.

None of those issues deterred David. He solved each problem before the plane landed in the US. But then he went the extra mile. When he learned the messenger had never been to the US before, David set up special transportation and arranged for someone to take him to a local baseball game so he could get his first taste of the States and so that he wouldn't be alone in a foreign country.

At the heart of the success of the company's change program were David and his colleagues. We treated each and every one of them like a CEO, walking them through a journey of recognizing how change would help them better fulfil their purposes. They each discovered their core cause and drove their actions in accordance with that internal compass. They were not defined by tools or software but rather by their commitment to make an impact on people's lives. It was that intrinsic motivation that inspired and empowered them to create amazing moments for their customers and be proud of what they were doing.

By helping each employee recognize the purpose and impact of the new system and by listening to their ideas about ways the organization could improve, the company was able to outperform its objectives and increase its overall change resilience.

HOW CHANGE RESILIENT ARE YOU?

Want a sense of your change resilience? A simple litmus test is to ask the following two questions:

- ✦ How quickly do I alter my behaviour when I know I need to change?

- ✦ Do I accept change reluctantly, or does it motivate me to take my work to the next level?

Keep in mind that we have a tendency to believe we are far more adaptable than we really are. Not sure about the answers? Want to know the truth? Ask a loved one to rank your willingness to try new food or music on a scale of 1 to 10 (1 = never, 10 = trying new things every day). Your colleagues or loved ones might be able to provide a more accurate mirror. (Just don't get insulted if they burst into laughter when you try to convince them that you really do love change...)

If you're assessing the change resilience of your organization, ask:

✦ The last time we introduced a new process or system, how long did it take to get every single person on board?

✦ What type of resistance (both passive and aggressive) did we experience in the process?

✦ How much time was spent to get buy-in and support?

✦ What was actually implemented versus what was planned?

✦ What did we have to give up from the original plan to please different stakeholders?

✦ Did our change program deliver the desired impact?

A start-up with 25 employees will likely have a high level of change resilience. Such a small and young organization has very little in the form of legacies and old practices. There are fewer employees to communicate with, and they are most likely all in one place. Therefore, any new initiative would be implemented rather quickly.

A 100-year-old global company with 50,000 employees, on the other hand, would have a very low change resilience level. Well-entrenched processes, old products and regional differences mean debates and delays that prevent a company from moving forward quickly.

But while some may argue that smaller organizations have an inherent advantage when it comes to change resilience, this is only partially true. Because of their small size and lack of resources, their change efforts will have limited impact. Larger organizations have a significant advantage there – they can lean on the legacy they've already built to rally their people for the next big win.

Combine the legacy and size of larger organizations with the nimbleness of smaller companies, and you've got the formula for optimal change resilience. It is not easy and it is not optional. But in a fast-changing world, change resilience is *the* competitive advantage.

Why Change?

"The Chicago market in particular, and the Midwest in general, just doesn't need these products."

That was what the Midwest chief sales manager declared, back in the days when I worked at Hewlett-Packard, when I asked him why our new security product had zero sales. As it turned out, he hadn't even tried to sell it.

"Besides, we made our numbers without the new security solution," he told me. "We don't need it."

"Well, it is not exactly our decision," I replied. "You are not in a position to determine the future of our division by avoiding selling our next-generation products and the key to our future market position."

My old colleague's unwillingness to adapt didn't just affect his numbers; by sticking to his old, soon-to-be-obsolete products, he put our entire growth and market strategy at risk.

He's hardly the only person I've encountered who's so focused on the day-to-day tasks that he can't see change approaching on the horizon. In fact, many people are reluctant to change because no one's properly explained *why* they need to change. If you find yourself in that position, consider the two major reasons change has become nonnegotiable in today's crowded markets:

1. **Change helps us defend a business position.**
   When markets grow more competitive or customers are losing interest, transformation can help you maintain your relevance and differentiate yourself. Refuse to change, and you risk accelerated commoditization.

2. **Change enables us to seize a new growth opportunity.** Expanding to new markets or introducing new products requires changing the way you do business. Avoid change, and you avoid growth.

If you feel that change is being thrust upon you arbitrarily, you probably just need more information. No one suggests change for the sake of change. We change to execute a vision, explore new opportunities, fulfil a dream. To stop change is to stop existence.

━━━ *CHANGE RESILIENCE CHALLENGE #3* ━━━

If your company is implementing a change, try this: ask your boss how she feels about it. You might find she was initially as surprised or frustrated as you are.

If you're leading a change and you haven't clearly and specifically told your employees why transformation is necessary, keep reading. Perhaps there was a time when people changed simply because their boss asked them to – but I guarantee you they probably weren't happy about it. These days, you run the risk of losing great people if you don't give them the opportunity to play a role in the change.

Change Resilience in a Crisis

It was a dark day for thousands of employees at the CPP Group when, in 2011, the Financial Services Authority, the British commission that governs financial services firms, decided to investigate the York-based credit card insurer.

The FSA had launched its investigation in response to several customer complaints and decided to do so with big public exposure.

As if the investigation itself wasn't bad enough, it was accompanied by newspaper headlines condemning CPP for unethical behaviour and consumer deception.

The accusations were harsh. Employees were blamed for skimming customers through aggressive and deceptive tactics. The company's stock tanked. Financing for the company became scarcer by the day. Thousands of families feared for their livelihood.

When we were called to assist in addressing the crisis, we personally reached out to more than 3,000 customers. We found out that the majority of them were very happy. Many were thankful to the company for its insurance and services. At the time, CPP served 11 million credit card holders and provided the assurance that if a card was stolen or lost, customers' lives would not be disrupted. Every day, CPP employees saved the day for honeymooners or family vacationers who lost their credit cards in foreign countries.

The demoralized workforce of CPP, however, didn't know any of that. They assumed that whatever was published in the press was true. They forgot the importance of what they really did and the impact they had on their customers' lives.

Our approach to help the company out of this crisis transferred employee focus from the investigation to the stories of customers they'd helped. We heavily emphasized the company's core cause:

"Helping the customer in need."

Insurance is an odd product – one you hope you never need to use. The only time you appreciate having insurance is when you're in trouble. It is at that moment when you need the full force of

CPP to replace your card, stop all fraudulent charges and assure you that you may continue your long-planned vacation. You can relax and enjoy the time with your family while CPP makes all the problems disappear.

By focusing employees on their core cause of helping customers, we helped them regain their pride. This boost in confidence gave them the change resilience they needed to continue meeting customer needs during a government investigation. Banks that were marketing their services were so impressed by CPP's ability to perform in a crisis that they decided to help finance the company. CPP not only survived – the company learned how to weather any crisis: by focusing on its purpose.

As we learned from our 2016 study with the *Harvard Business Review*, companies fail to change when people aren't connected to the change or fail to understand its purpose. The new system or program seems like another shiny new management toy. Why waste their time?

Helping employees see the connection between change and their core cause is the antidote to this lack of engagement. Remember that a core cause isn't about *you* – it's about the impact you're making on another person. An organization's core cause should be defined from the customer's perspective. And we cannot declare victory until customers confirm that they have, in fact, been positively impacted.

It is at that moment when you think *customer* before you think *process* that you can connect to your purpose and understand your impact.

=== *CHANGE RESILIENCE CHALLENGE #4* ===

What are your customers' dreams and aspirations? If you know the answer to that question – and can connect your actions to these aspirations – you will be more intrinsically motivated to do your work and better able to weather any change that comes your way.

The Language of Change

If you want to examine change at its highest level, check out Kickstarter. The crowdfunding site features new ideas from all kinds of creators: from up-and-coming musicians and designers to inventors and entrepreneurs seeking seed money. This site is all about selling the Next and convincing people to invest in a change yet to happen. If an idea strikes a chord, the level of interest can be staggering – even to the creators. Take Pebble, the e-paper watch – 18,000 people backed what was originally a $100,000 campaign. Funding hit $2.6 million in just three days.

Tanushree Mitra and Eric Gilbert of the Georgia Institute of Technology recently conducted a study whose aim was to identify the key phrases and words associated with the most successful Kickstarter campaigns. After studying some 20,000 phrases in 45,000 campaigns, their conclusion was striking. They split the most successful phrases into four categories:

1. **Reciprocity** – Successful projects created a sense that, by supporting the project, backers were entering into a relationship with the creators.

2. **Scarcity** – When there was a limit on the number of products or rewards available, a project appealed to backers who wanted to be part of the 'in crowd'.

3. **Social Proof** – Backers were drawn to products they felt had some sort of social benefit.

4. **Social Identity** – The idea that a certain product would establish you in a social group played an important role in getting backers on board.

There's a compelling pattern here: three out of the four categories of the most successful phrases emphasized selflessness, impact on others and connection. Whether knowingly or not, Kickstarter backers responded favourably when pitches emphasized social impact and reciprocity. Campaigns that highlighted selfish, individual benefits simply didn't deliver the same level of success.

This study provides compelling evidence that people are willing to take a chance on change if there are social benefits to doing so. It stands in stark contrast to popular wisdom about change – for example, that a fear of embarrassment holds people back from changing.

This is exactly why a core cause is so important.

When it comes to our ability to absorb and adapt to change, knowing that the change will better allow us to help others is *the* key driver. Strengthening your relationships with those affected by the change will accelerate your commitment to personal and professional transformation.

Evolve, Don't Change

By viewing change through the lens of the core cause, we downgrade the importance of each process or tool. We focus instead on who we are and what we stand for. We focus on that which stays constant even when everything else in the world appears to be changing.

At this point, you may be asking, "Well, if my core cause stays the same, what is this transformation I'm supposed to be embracing?"

Evolution.

Evolution means continually adapting and responding to new opportunities. Of course, not every opportunity is worth pursuing. But an understanding of your core cause will help you recognize which ones are.

I hope by now you've had an *Aha!* moment:

By retaining a strong commitment to your values, you make yourself future ready.

I know that when this insight hit me, I felt it was BIG. When I began sharing it with people, I noticed how it relaxed them. It validated what they'd done in the past – whatever change they were about to undertake was not a punishment for failure. Their previous successes were real, and they deserved recognition.

Thinking about change in this way frees people up to view an upcoming transformation in a more balanced and open-minded way. Transformation is no longer threatening. Their identity remains intact.

This is the foundation that change resilience is built on. With a strong and stable understanding of our purpose, we can adapt to any change – provided the alignment is right. We can then approach change from a position of power. Change becomes a tool to enhance our skills, not replace them.

It sparks the question: what are you waiting for?

two

FEAR OF CHANGE

The World Is Always Changing. Are You?

Picture a small, brightly lit conference room. A dozen employees sit around a few tables, ready for a change management workshop. On a long table at the back are a couple of urns of coffee, a stack of Styrofoam cups and two large platters of stale pastries.

Typical workshop, right?

Now, picture those same employees leaping to their feet in anger, faces purple, shouting and hurling insults at the top of their lungs. Picture them doing that for two solid hours.

The object of their rage? Me – the guy presenting at the front of the room. You'll recognize me by my futile attempts to regain control of the situation. It seems funny in retrospect, but it wasn't at the time. I was legitimately scared. It was arguably one of the most violent change workshops I had ever led. Participants even made verbal threats toward me in full view of management.

"We know people like you," they told me.

"We're watching you," they said.

It was clear they felt they had nothing to lose, and it occurred to me at one point that if things got physical, I'd get no sympathy. Face down a biker gang and you can hold your head a little higher in that full-body cast. Face down the employees of an auto dealership in a conference room? Not so much.

I left the workshop shaken and scared. Some of the employees came up to me afterward to apologize, but that didn't do much to settle my nerves.

Given their behaviour, it might surprise you to learn they actually recognized that the change I was suggesting was necessary to catch up with their competitors. It might also surprise you to know the change I was suggesting: providing their customers with express car service. Yes, that's it. Customers were requesting faster turnaround – a service their competitors were already offering.

The employees in the workshop were reasonable, experienced professionals, so why were they resisting such a logical change? Well, they had a multitude of reasons – excuses ranging from changes in the work schedule to compensation shifts they believed would result from working differently. All of the rational arguments I had prepared to address each concern seemed to fall on deaf ears. They refused to listen.

In other words, their response was totally illogical.

The question is: Why? The facts to support the change were very clear and quite compelling. The change was not going to be difficult to implement. It wasn't a case of a lack of resources or of laziness either. These were well-intentioned, hardworking people who were proud of their work and the service they provided.

And still, they were not future ready.

What I was seeing was not unique. When looking back at all the transformational projects I've been involved in, one thing is clear: people's responses to change have nothing to do with logic. We're hardwired to hold on to the Now instead of embracing the Next. After all, the Now is comforting and predictable. We do not want to leave this presumably safe, familiar place. It is reassuring and comforting. Losing it is like losing a piece of ourselves.

The Next, on the other hand, is hard. Why? In a word: *fear*. Anything that deviates from the status quo scares people. We reflexively resist new ideas and new ways of doing things because we cling to the past. For an individual who hasn't developed change resilience, even a small change can trigger an existential crisis.

I meet people struggling with this every day. Believe it or not, you can see the signs of agitation in their eyes. These people are experiencing genuine panic over something as innocuous as the implementation of a new fulfilment system or a modification to the company's reimbursement policy. What's going on here?

Psychologists will tell you that these employees are in fight-or-flight mode. After all, the typical human response to change is anxiety. When the human body experiences fear, the brain releases potent chemicals into the bloodstream to help us either defeat the threat or turn tail and run for the bushes. This instinctive response is useful when there's a bear in your campsite – not so much at 9:30am Monday morning in conference room C. Fight-or-flight brings increased strength and endurance, and quicker response time. The one thing it *doesn't* amplify is rational thought.

I've run some tough sessions in my career. My teams have engaged with more than a million employees at organizations ranging from government agencies serving citizens and cruise lines delighting vacationers to logistics operators managing overnight shipments and healthcare providers treating life-threatening conditions. Every transformation effort is different and introducing change is never easy. The workshop I described at the start of the chapter, however, was on another level. The raw emotion and resistance were like nothing I'd ever experienced. While the participants acknowledged that the service would help them against the competition, customers wanted it and something along these lines was necessary, *this* change had to be stopped.

I can imagine you're shaking your head right now.

Come on, Lior, you're thinking. *I'm not like those people. Sure, I've resisted change in the past. I may even be pushing back right now. But* my *reasons for resisting change are always legitimate, logical and reasonable. These people were clearly just ... crazy.*

But they weren't.

What could lead reasonable, experienced professionals to aggressively resist a logical improvement, one that had become standard in the industry, one that customers now demanded?

To be fair, they had their reasons. Unfortunately, their reasons weren't very logical. Here's a rundown:

+ **"Management will never fully support these changes."** In fact, management had already invested hundreds of thousands of dollars in new equipment and process redesign.

+ **"This is just the program-du-jour. We have a track record of launch-and-abandon."** Management was committed to some major structural changes, and employees knew it. In fact, the dealership was due to begin constructing a permanent interior installation, featuring newly designed signage, the day after I left. Such investment does not represent a launch-and-abandon mentality.

+ **"Our customers don't want that."** All their competitors already offered this service, so it was pretty clear customers *did* want it.

+ **"This will mess up the work schedule."** Yes, the new express service would change the work schedule, but for the better. Because express work was an optional choice for customers and would be handled separately, workers would have more flexibility when it came to important but nonurgent work.

✦ **"This is going to affect my paycheck."**
In fact, the new express car service offering
would take low-margin services such as oil
changes off employees' plates, freeing them to
focus on more profitable, large-ticket services
that they'd previously had to refuse or refer
elsewhere due to lack of resources.

✦ **"They will outsource our work to less-
qualified technicians."** Yes, the change would
require additional labor, but every profession has
degrees of specialization and, with time, every
employee gains more expertise. By fighting the
natural expansion of offerings, they were destroying the dealership's ability to grow and evolve.

All my responses to these concerns were met with grimaces, crossed
arms and blank stares. They didn't just refuse to listen – they couldn't
hear me at all. Their fear was too loud. Eventually, the shouting began.

The employees at the dealership demonstrated a remarkable lack
of change resilience. But their negative reaction wasn't truly unusual.
Dial it down from a ten to a seven, and you have an example of the
typical employee reaction to a change effort. Every time I work with
a new company, I meet smart people who are generally proud of
what they do. They want to do good work and serve the customer,
but they still fail to adapt and stay relevant.

Why?

Few words in the English language conjure both fear and excitement the way *change* does. We might get excited about something new, but we can't help but fear the mistakes we're sure to make, the uncertainty involved.

Change, in other words, is terrific – as long as we don't need to do any changing ourselves.

Everyone wants to reap the benefits of a positive improvement, but people still resist letting go of old behaviours in order to make room for new ones. They'd prefer that transformation be painless, fast and immediately rewarding. A quick trip to the Promised Land without the jet lag or the turbulence. We want to break one of life's cardinal rules: "No pain, no gain." Since we can't come out and admit a motive so childish, we rationalize our delays or idealize the past:

"New is not necessarily good."

"How come no one else is doing it?"

"What's so bad about the way we do it now?"

"Go prove it with others first."

"My customers are *different*."

"There is no need for a solution because there isn't a genuine problem."

"If there were really a need for it, someone else would have invented it already."

"Give me a few more days/weeks/months/years."

"My grandmother lived to a 102 without it."

These are all ways to avoid saying what we really mean: "I don't want to change." I have heard all of these excuses – and many more.

If you've ever tried to implement change, you've heard some of them too. Anyone who's tried to change has likely come face-to-face with the incredible hidden strength of the human spirit: we are amazingly crafty and tenacious when it comes to resisting change and holding on to old behaviours. Sometimes we even hold fast to the tried-and-true while preaching change to others!

Given the speed and scope of change today, we simply don't have time for these excuses anymore. This pervasive lack of change resilience has a real and tangible impact on organizations:

+ For one leading US credit card company, we identified $20 million of additional customer charges a month if they delighted only 5% of their unhappy customers. (Imagine the financial impact if they delighted more than 5%!)

+ For a global over-the-counter pharmaceutical manufacturer, we identified a loss of $104 million for every 1% loss in customer satisfaction.

+ A manufacturer that refused to change its invoicing practice discovered that the outdated method was costing $21 million a year.

And on and on. Change represents an opportunity to either increase revenue or decrease costs. When change is delayed, losses mount.

Yet most employees still fall back on a multitude of tricks to avoid change at all costs, paying lip service to it and then abandoning it when no one is looking. It all comes down to fear.

"What I say"

FUTURE-BASED FEAR
"What will it be like?"
"How will I do it?"
"Will I fail to adapt?"

"What I really think"

PAST-BASED FEAR
"What does it mean about my past?"
"Was everything up until now a mistake?"
"How do I relate to my past?"

IDENTITY-BASED FEAR
"How does change impact my values?"
"What does the change make me?"
"How does it change who I am?"

As the diagram illustrates, the top of the pyramid reflects the type of change resistance that's most visible. For example, people will frequently express concerns about the future such as, "What will it be like?" Such statements, however, are deceiving. If you attempt to address them, you will miss the deeper, underlying issues. Underneath every future-based fear, there are two deeper fears: fears rooted in the past, and fears triggered by the challenge to one's identity. When people are stuck in the past, they struggle with how to contextualize their past performance with a need for change. They need to place their performance in a positive light before they can engage with the future-based fears. Identity-based fear takes this a step deeper. Often people feel that the upcoming change is a threat to who they are and not just what they do. They struggle with more existential questions about the impact of the future on their values and how they define themselves. Addressing those deeper fears is essential to preparing for the future.

The Judgment of the Past

Let's look at a very real and very significant example of disruptive change in action.

Sweden is rapidly becoming a cashless society. One in five transactions happens digitally (the vast majority are credit-card based), and cash payments amount to less than 2% of the value of all payments in the country. Retailers aren't required to accept physical currency and many don't, preferring payment by credit card or smartphone. Swedes can't even use cash to pay for public transportation and many other key services.

As a result, many Swedish banks no longer keep cash on hand or allow deposits. ATMs are vanishing rapidly. Most financial transactions of any kind are completed electronically, and the trend is only accelerating. Within five years, cash will be a thing of the past in Sweden.

Such a radical shift poses a serious threat to, let's say, a 20-year bank veteran who believes her job is to accept and dispense cash.

To an ATM engineer tasked with installing and maintaining these soon-to-be-extinct machines, this is a crisis.

Change initiatives are always presented as the Next Big Thing, announced with much fanfare as the big breakthrough we've all been waiting for. For employees, however, these initiatives read as an assault on their hard work. Past achievements are being painted, in retrospect, as archaic, inadequate failures.

CHANGE RESILIENCE CHALLENGE #5

When announcing a new change, don't forget to celebrate the past and acknowledge the hard work it took to get where you are. A change shouldn't be an assault on the past – it's a way to build on a legacy.

For a Swedish bank teller with decades of experience at the counter, cashless banking tells her: "You're useless." She will struggle to reconcile the hard work she has invested over the years with the shiny new technology that renders all of it obsolete. She will wrestle with accepting what is, to everyone else, an unambiguous improvement.

Typical change initiatives are so preoccupied with celebrating the future that they fail to recognize the importance of the past and those who laboured to get the organization here. It is only when we respectfully acknowledge the significance of the past that we begin to get people unstuck. This requires proactive communication and a genuine understanding of the history of the organization leading up to the change.

If you're leading a change program at your organization, it's your job to make people comfortable by creating a meaningful transition between the past and the future. If you're an employee tasked with adapting to a new change, you have the opportunity to help your colleagues and customers embrace the change by demonstrating the connection between the past you've lived and the future you will build.

We'll dive deeper into exactly how to do this in the pages that follow – and I'll address exactly how to face all the fears you or the ones you love may be having about a looming change. For now, what's important is to remember that change is not a complete break with the past, and it's certainly not a dismissal of anyone's hard work or past achievement.

WHAT'S YOUR EXPERIENCE WITH CHANGE?

Many people reject change because their previous experiences with it have been so negative. So let's take a moment to get clear about any preconceived notions you might have when it comes to change. Ask yourself:

✦ The last time you made a major change, were you excited or reluctant about it?

> ✦ Take a look at the software or communication
>   tools that you're using. Were you planning to
>   adopt that new technology? Did you embrace
>   it immediately? Or was it something that you
>   were dragged into?
>
> ✦ If you were dragged into making a change,
>   why was this the case? What was your ini-
>   tial reaction?

How Would Change Liberate You?

When working with employees around digital transformation, it's very easy to see the sadness in their eyes. They recognize the need to adapt, but deep down they fear that they are being replaced. They see the relationship with technology as a zero-sum game in which every advancement makes them a little less valuable. While they know that customers seek new technological solutions, they feel marginalized in the process. Their life's work is being reduced to an iPhone app, diminishing the value they used to create for their customers.

To them, change is an existential threat.

When I work with teams that are being asked to adapt to new technology, I ask, "How much value do you add by filling out forms for a customer?" Often, this question helps them reframe the situation. What they failed to see was that the technology was actu-ally liberating them from this chore, freeing them up to spend more time adding value to their customers' lives. Now they have much more time to consult, advise and, ultimately, help people make the right decisions.

Change usually opens up new opportunities. That's why we should ask the following questions whenever facing a new change:

+ How does the change impact or support my core cause?

+ What do I need to *stop doing* as a result of the change?

+ What time/resources/mindset will I gain from making this change?

+ How does the change liberate me to pursue my core cause?

With Change Comes Responsibility

Let's be honest about why change is so scary. As technology evolves, it *does* render certain kinds of jobs obsolete. New jobs are created, and they usually demand skills that those in eliminated positions don't yet possess. All too often, companies fail to put a plan in place to help employees evolve into these new roles. So people who have long identified their worth with their work find themselves cast adrift, desperately seeking a role – and a new identity.

Is it any wonder that so many of us are scared of change?

Before we completed our research into this phenomenon, I often wondered how rational and intelligent people could make such sloppy and irrational arguments against obvious improvements. Today, I have a much better idea why people resist the inevitable.

If you're unsure why those around you are having such a difficult time embracing a new change, read on. This methodology is a step-by-step plan for involving everyone in the process of change: after all, change shouldn't be an excuse to leave people behind. Just as managers expect employees to stay current with the demands of their industries, managers have a responsibility to involve their employees in the evolution of their companies.

And if you're worried that shifts in the economy or your industry are putting your job in danger, take heart. Notice that I said that change renders certain 'roles' obsolete. But what it can't destroy is the need to provide high-quality services to people in need.

The Personalities of Change Rejection

Like opera, change rejection is an art, one that has been perfected by the human spirit. Just when you think you've covered all the arguments, someone will miraculously discover a new aria to lengthen the final act another few bars. It's astonishing – and infuriating too, if you're the one trying to make change happen.

While the excuses themselves will vary by company and industry, I have identified six common change rejection 'personalities'.

When encountering resistance – whether your own or someone else's – it's incredibly helpful to identify which one you're dealing with, because each personality responds better to different approaches.

You're probably unaware of the many small ways you put up resistance. Diagnosing your change rejection personality can open a window into your unconscious behaviours and offer a path toward solutions.

I. The Staller

Nothing in this meeting should be coming as a surprise to anyone. All the relevant stakeholders have reviewed the latest customer study. Everyone knows the severity of the customer issues and the consequences of not taking action immediately. We have gathered this morning solely to sign off on the new strategy. Yet, as we cover the core findings one last time and begin to review everyone's next actions, Chris, a marketing director, speaks up.

"The numbers are conclusive," he declares cheerfully. "They leave no doubt about what needs to happen next."

Then, the punch line.

"Just to make sure, though, would you mind running the numbers one more time in a slightly different way?"

Every team has a marketing director named Chris who decides at the last minute that he wants to compare the data from single women over the age of 50 in southern Florida with what we have from young families in Seattle. Chris is one of the six types of change rejecters: the staller. Chris will never object to the data per se.

You can't argue with the facts, right? Instead, he will innocently dig his heels in using tactics like this and make you drag him the rest of the way.

Back to the meeting. Here's how I worked with Chris's resistance – and how you can handle your own staller.

Shutting Down the Staller: What's the Cost of the Delay?

In the interests of consensus, the project champion looks ready to agree to Chris's request for additional analysis. Time for me to step in.

"What are you trying to establish that isn't in the report already?" I ask. "And how would you measure the cost of delaying the original plan against the added value of any new information you might find?"

Silence in the room. Chris was counting on his colleagues to let him get away with stalling once again. He certainly wasn't expecting a challenge.

"We have frustrated customers," I add, in the hope of restoring the sense of urgency in the room. "Every day we leave them that way is another day they can shop around with our competitors."

Chris's forced cheerfulness evaporates.

"Okay," he responds, defeated. "Let's do it."

The staller's fear is simple: the proposed change might uncover that he didn't do his job as well as he could have or neglected something critical. Stalling the change effort is his last desperate bid to protect his reputation. This was why Chris was so resistant. He'd made some mistakes in the past – and the proposed change was going to bring them to light.

The best way to handle a silent delayer is to dig deep into these additional requests by asking questions like:

- ✦ Why do we need more information?

- ✦ How will what we might learn affect the proposed change?

- ✦ Will the additional value offset the cost of the delay?

Don't play nice with the staller. Instead, emphasize the very real damage that delays will have on your overall strategy. If you know you have a staller in your midst, approach him in advance to address these issues in a way that minimizes the damage to him and to the change effort. Even better, find new opportunities for the staller to own the new change instead of fearing it.

On encountering one staller, my team discovered that he was afraid of the additional work that the new program would add to his plate. He was comfortable in his marketing role – his department activated many fun sponsorships that afforded him trips to glitzy events. The new program and additional responsibility meant fewer fun events and more customer interactions, something he wasn't looking forward to. We presented a compromise: a new reduced role that would allow him to stay involved with sponsorships while a new director of marketing was appointed.

2. The Engineer

"These customers are stupid," he repeated angrily. "They just don't bother to read the manual."

He was one of my R&D managers at Hewlett-Packard. An engineer through and through, he was in love with his products. Generally speaking, engineers don't like change – unless it's on their terms. They also tend to suffer from acute NIHS: Not Invented Here Syndrome. For someone with NIHS, the only thing better than a good idea is his idea.

"We show your products to everyone," I replied. "Apparently, only the stupid ones actually buy them. So until I get different products, we're stuck serving stupid customers."

The engineer – who doesn't, of course, have to be an *actual* engineer – is very open to change, as long as it's *her change*. Unfortunately, there is no room for this kind of monomaniacal thinking in today's world – not even if you're the CEO. Good ideas come from everywhere – and sometimes someone else has a more appropriate solution than we do. To adapt, people need to be ready to embrace the optimal approach regardless of its provenance.

The engineer shuns risk. She is most comfortable with the clear, the proven and the predictable. But change is often none of those things.

Changing the Engineer's Mind: Make the Case

If you're an engineer or you're trying to convince one of the need for change, it's time to do some research. Prove beyond a shadow of a doubt that the old way is no longer valid. Engineers are more likely to accept that innovation is necessary if your case is made with copious rigor and detail. Give them (or yourself) all the facts they can stand in order to activate their change resilience.

It's also helpful to develop a set of milestones for change. This systematic approach reassures the engineer that data will continue to be collected, analysed and incorporated along the way.

3. The Busy Bee

"Are you kidding me? I don't have time for change! I'm needed in five different places right this very minute. In fact, I've received more than 50 critical emails since we started talking."

The busy bee is the manager with too much on his plate. Sometimes it seems as if his chief responsibility is to convince everyone else of his importance to the organization. The company's very survival depends on him – or at least, he'd like people to think so. The busy bee's typical response to a change effort is contempt: "I can't be bothered worrying about the future when I'm playing such an instrumental role in closing the quarter!"

The busy bee is afraid of losing his prominence in the organization. He puts out fires; saving the day constantly garners him respect. This change on the horizon may cause the busy bee to lose his privileged spot by extinguishing those fires for good. How will he prove his worth then?

The busy bee uses today's problems as an excuse not to deal with tomorrow's crisis. Often he runs a chaotic department in operations or customer service, one lacking any real structure. This chaos feeds the busy-ness that makes him feel needed and important.

Bringing the Busy Bee on Board: Make Her Life Easier

The busy-ness, though manufactured, is still real. If the presence of an obviously distracted and overwhelmed busy bee is derailing your change effort, assess how much you really need to include her in the process.

If you can get started elsewhere and get back to her once you've built up momentum, do so. Otherwise, use the change as a vehicle to improve her operation and create more structure and effectiveness there. If you can show the busy bee that change is not something being layered on top of what she does but rather a smoother alternative, you may have a shot.

If *you're* the bee, ask yourself: Do I really need to put up so much resistance? Can I take some time during one of my quieter moments to better understand the change? You may find it can make life easier once you get past the initial learning curve.

Make no mistake, however: busy bees need systems that give them as many opportunities as possible to solve problems, earn respect and feel important. They thrive on adrenaline, but successful, positive change can deliver similar thrills if they're open to it.

4. The Salesperson

"But I made my numbers the old way!"

This is the cry of the salesperson, another classic change rejecter. Often this person literally works in sales – but not always. The salesperson is anyone who regularly declares victory for making monthly, quarterly and annual quotas. She will actively resist anything that might put her predictable revenue streams and juicy commissions in jeopardy.

For the salesperson, change is first and foremost a threat to the revenue stream. As she sees it, change means greater risk and longer sales cycles. She will do her best to keep change far away from her territory and minimize any disruption to her hard-earned track record. Any proposed change will threaten the company's revenues, its stock price, its very existence.

The salesperson follows a peculiar logic all her own. "I'm happy to change," she might say. "We just need to renegotiate my quota for the year. I have no intention of losing my target commission and my place in the President's Club trip. So as long as you can guarantee that all the risks involved in this change are off my plate, I'm in."

This attitude deals the death blow to your change program. There are no guarantees in any change, and the salesperson knows it. By shifting responsibility to everyone else, she is protecting herself at the cost of the company's future.

The fear here is simple: loss of money and status. Salespeople have a formula for success. They follow it, make their numbers and reap the rewards. Messing with their formula endangers their standing. Because of their direct impact on overall revenue, salespeople often have the clout to fight change to a standstill. In fact, many organizations try to sidestep sales entirely when it comes to change. They will ask me to approach sales last during the change process. While this is sometimes an option, more often it is not.

Celebrating the Salesperson: Create a New Formula for Success

The way to handle the salesperson is through the CEO. You'll need the CEO's unconditional buy-in and support to effectively tell the sales department – or anyone charged with hitting some sort of quota – to stop playing the oldest game in the book. The CEO must establish the change effort as the top priority and refuse to accept any ultimatums. Yes, there are ways to minimize the risks to immediate revenues due to new programs; but at the same time salespeople should refrain from inflating the risks they do face just to stop the change at any cost.

Don't let the salesperson get away with using outlier examples to make general objections to the plan. Focus on addressing what *will* work in most instances and worry about exceptions later.

If you're the salesperson, then you know well what motivates you. It may help to create a new formula to define success and talk to your colleagues about it. You've been trained to be reward-driven, so celebrate successes early and often. Between progress-based rewards and new opportunities for elevated status, you can overcome your natural resistance to change.

5. The Silo Builder

Change requires sharing. Change requires collaboration. Change requires a willingness to be measured together, not individually. You can't hide behind your personal or team performance at everyone else's expense. To a silo builder, change is a threat to his carefully cultivated turf.

The silo builder wants to be judged on his own merits and has no intention of standing with the team. He will maintain the walls of separation within the organization and oppose any changes to them. He will rationalize his stance by talking about accountability: "By increasing collaboration and breaking down silos, how will you hold people *accountable*? Change will only breed chaos."

What the silo builder *really* fears is increased responsibility. If you've been managing a small, well-controlled process, it's scary to consider becoming responsible for a broader program where you can't control every aspect yourself. Collaboration means depending on others who might fail.

Soothe the Silo Builder's Fears: Emphasize Organizational Accountability

While assuring the silo builder that accountability is a good thing, emphasize that no man is an island. Each person is ultimately responsible for executing the company's strategy and delivering superior value to customers. Like it or not, everyone is in this *together*. It doesn't matter if one person meets his numbers if he does so at the expense of everyone else in the organization. Allowing individual accountability to trump the organization's larger strategy impairs everyone's efforts.

Assure silo builders that the proposed change will drive organizational accountability. Point out the differences between micro and macro accountability, and tally the costs of following a short-sighted, micro-only approach.

If you're the silo builder, it's your job to strengthen your relationships with others. Think about times when someone from another department really came through for you. Remember a moment when a team member helped you do a more effective job. Deep down, you know that you can't do the work alone. The good news is: you don't have to.

Underneath all the so-called rational arguments against change you will find emotional motives. Ignoring the emotional impact change has on people will only result in increasingly creative methods of sabotage. Only when we understand the different forms resistance takes can we develop the change resilience we need to bring our organizations into the future.

Which brings us to the sixth change rejecter, someone who is perhaps the least invested in making the changes necessary for evolution:

6. The Veteran

The veteran is two or three years away from retirement. She's not looking to make any waves, and change is *not* a part of her retirement plan. She plans to keep things just the way they are, thank you very much.

There are some ways to appeal to the veteran. You may focus on the legacy she will leave behind. For those who are very proud of their work and intrinsically motivated, this approach may work. In other cases, you may want to break the required operational changes into small, bite-size activities that may seem less daunting. A combination of intrinsic motivation and bite-size changes may be appropriate for some veterans.

But in some instances, the best way to ensure a change initiative's success is to begin it the day after the veteran's retirement party. Considering that every day you postpone change is a day you lose more money, you may even consider expediting that party. Despite all the organization's appreciation for past performance, it cannot afford to allow one person's love of the past to hold everyone else's future hostage. In some cases, change resilience is about letting go of those who refuse to take the next step in the journey. That can be scary – but as we've seen in this chapter, change is all about courage in the face of fear.

If you're a veteran reading this book, then I believe you care about your work and your legacy. You may need to swallow your pride and ask for assistance embracing the Next, but the payoff is worth it.

The Emotions That Drive Change

When a Korean-based global manufacturer announced that it would enter the high-end segment of its market, the responses were less than enthusiastic. Far less, to be honest. When soliciting advice from experts as to how to go about it, they were told: "Give customers coupons."

It seemed everyone was looking forward to seeing the company fail.

After all, they were still a relatively new brand – one known for low-cost, low-excitement products. Theirs were the products for those who couldn't afford more expensive brands.

While the company had already introduced more sophisticated models that were priced about 50% higher than their typical products, producing and selling a product that cost *twice as much* as anything they'd made before was far beyond anyone's imagination.

To test the company's readiness for selling a high-end product, we sent out mystery shoppers to retailers offering some of the early high-end models. To our amazement, when our shoppers pushed hard on the price, salespeople proposed something we had never heard before. They offered to replace the company's emblem with a nondescript logo so "no one will know you are using this product."

This level of lack of pride and belief in the product was shocking – definitely not a good foundation for leaping into the high-end space.

When we tested the concept in focus groups with salespeople, they dismissed the idea of moving into the high-end segment. They did not see why people would buy the new product when they could buy an established, proven high-end product. "It is not who we are," they said. "This is not our market." They could see starting a new brand dedicated to luxury models, but did not see any value in extending the existing product line into the luxury space.

But for this company, introducing a premium product was not just a whim. It was a strategic move – not only did the company's leadership want to cover a complete lineup of offerings, they wanted to grow with customers as they grew in age and affluence. They wanted to develop an integrated approach that kept customers for life. The problem? No one, including the company's own salespeople, believed in this strategy.

While the reactions to the change *seemed* logical, they were in fact more emotional than they might appear. There was a strong cynical voice in customers' and salespeople's heads, telling them:

"This is not us. This is not who we are. This is not our identity and personality."

If we wanted to move forward with the strategic change, we needed to confront this personality crisis head-on. This became a much bigger issue than moving into a new market. It was putting people's core convictions and sense of identity and purpose to the test.

Before developing the new blueprint for how to execute this market extension, we needed to develop a narrative to preempt the cynical voice. We had to reestablish the company's personality – and we needed to start with the employees.

The answer was Bold Forward, a theme-based internal campaign and brand training that we designed to reframe the company as a bold player in an industry full of old thinkers. We helped reposition the manufacturer as a challenger that would appeal to customers seeking a product that was edgier and cool. Leveraging success stories from the company's past, we developed a personality that was authentic and relatable. Combined with new behaviours and practices that were instilled during special workshops, we were able to accomplish the mission. Within six months, the new high-end product was being sold at full price. No longer were retailers or employees apologizing for their brand; they were proud to talk about what it was and what it stood for.

This is one of the truly exciting aspects of change – and it's one that applies equally to individuals. Change can be uncomfortable because it means growing into who you really are. But instead of being proud of who we are and what we are, individuals and companies alike often compare themselves to others. If you find yourself in this position, consider the words of Oscar Wilde: "Be yourself. Everyone else is already taken."

Management by Butterflies in the Stomach

A final note about fear: while it's true that we don't want our fear of change to paralyze us or hold us back, a little anxiety can actually be a good thing. In fact, I often call my leadership style "management by butterflies in the stomach."

In other words, if you've lost the butterflies-in-your-stomach feeling when it comes to your work, you're on autopilot. You will take people for granted. You're acting as a process operator, not a high-impact performer.

When you operate on autopilot, you take your customers for granted. You assume you already have the answer to their wishes and do not engage in exploration of what they truly need. This is a rule that I adapted when I speak in public. The day I lose the butterflies in my stomach is the day I know I will fail. Because the alternative – being on autopilot – means neglecting or taking for granted the audience that came to hear me.

Think about it: Why do so many of us have anxiety? Because we're afraid to fail. And we're not just afraid of letting ourselves down – we usually don't want to disappoint someone else. We recognize that there is someone on the other side of our work. We know that what we do matters.

When you drop the anxiety, when you no longer have a few butterflies floating around, you become like the singer who rests on the laurels of his biggest hit or a stand-up comic who tells the same jokes over and over. A little bit of fear can be your secret weapon. It's not your weakness, it's your power. It keeps you aware. It keeps you focused. It keeps you thinking about what's Next.

three

THE SECRET TO CHANGE RESILIENCE: ENGAGEMENT

Beyond Inspiration, Discipline

When Stanford University's Professor Sebastian Thrun made his artificial intelligence course available via online broadcast in 2011, he had no idea of the ripple effect it was about to cause. The course was viewed by more than 160,000 people and promised to revolutionize higher education.

Massive open online courses (MOOCs), online courses open to anyone, emerged as a popular method of learning just one year later. Professor Thrun himself was energized and started Udacity that same year. The goal? To make academic content available to anyone who sought to elevate themselves. Competing platforms such as Coursera, edX, Khan Academy, and iversity followed suit. The hype was substantial. Once again the internet was democratizing access and making knowledge available, free of charge. All you needed to bring was your interest.

Two years later, things looked a little different.

A 2013 study showed that only 5% of the students in 17 Coursera classes offered through the University of Pennsylvania actually finished their classes. Similar studies demonstrated that the edX platform at Harvard and MIT did not fare much better.

What was even more concerning was that the students who *did* complete the classes were usually those with prior higher education experience, not the intended target of the MOOC revolution. Individuals with weaker education backgrounds failed to take full advantage of MOOCs. Realizing this, Thrun admitted in a *Fast Company* interview, "I have a lousy product."

So what happened?

Unfortunately, availability and interest do not always equal usability and commitment. Just because a student was initially interested in enrolling doesn't mean that interest will be sufficient to get him or her to complete the course. In other words, the classes offered by these platforms lacked several elements required to help people become more change resilient:

1. **Context was not provided.** Students signed up for courses out of general interest but did not have a reason for committing to complete them. There is a huge difference between the kind of interest sparked by watching a YouTube demo video and a commitment to months of disciplined learning and exercises.

2. **There was no financial investment.** Free is just that: free. Because there was no penalty for dropping courses, students demonstrated no real commitment to sticking with them. Many probably joined just because it was free.

3. **There was a lack of discipline.** The success of MOOCs relied on the sheer willpower of the students to carry them through. As the study showed, only 5% of students were able to complete a course thanks to sheer willpower – and most of those students were highly educated people who'd been trained in self-discipline.

If you want to transform interest and inspiration into lifelong action, you need context, discipline and consequences. In other words, interest in a subject won't translate into commitment unless it is coupled with real engagement.

Are You Engaged?

If you're currently resisting a change, ask yourself: Am I truly engaged with the process or its proposed outcome? Be honest. If you don't know the answer, here are some other questions to ask:

+ When asked to make a change, do I think creatively about how to approach it? If I'm driving the change at my organization, do I ask employees for their ideas?

+ When charged with making a decision or solving a problem, would I prefer to defer to my managers so I'm not held responsible? Do I give my employees opportunities to solve problems related to change?

Much like good customer service, creativity around change cannot be dictated from the top. Employees need to personally decide to change – and to think creatively about how to change. A paycheck only buys your employees' passive attendance – but compliance isn't enough. You need engagement.

The Secret to Employee Engagement

In May 2016, Strativity launched a nationwide study of 30,183 adults, employed full- or part-time, in an attempt to better understand employee engagement. We gave participants a list of statements in order to explore what factors played the biggest role when it came to engagement at work – and, by extension, their readiness and willingness to change and adapt. (From previous work, we had already learned that engaged employees demonstrate a greater willingness to adapt to change.) Here's what we discovered:

- Only 31% of employees agreed that "our company's leaders inspire me to follow them."

- Only 34% said, "my direct supervisor inspires me."

- Just 37% believed "this job is aligned with my career goals."

- The same proportion, just 37%, could say, "my direct supervisor helps me develop my skills."

- Finally, only 38% felt that "I have complete ownership of the issues I deal with."

As bad as the scores were, what else we discovered about them might surprise you: none of these factors had any clear correlation to engagement – or lack thereof.

In fact, each of the needs expressed in the above statements was perceived by employees to be a basic requirement. So what else could be responsible for engagement? Education or income level? Think again. Neither had any link to engagement.

As it turned out, the strongest correlation to engagement was demonstrated by three statements that comprise what we call the Impact Index:

1. "Our leaders inspire me to follow them."

2. "I understand our customers' needs and expectations."

3. "Our company's leaders effectively communicate with me."

What is so special about these statements? In fact, several things. While other factors the employees rated treated them in a passive way – statements such as "Work/life balance" – the Impact Index statements focused on the employee as an active participant. While others focused on the big picture – "Competitive strategy," for instance – which some employees may feel is too big for them to influence, these statements focused on the power that employees *do* have.

When people are inspired to act, understand the need they are addressing for their customer and have their role in making an impact clearly communicated, they are ready to make a difference.

In other words, people demonstrate the highest engagement not when their personal needs are being met, but rather when they feel empowered to make an impact and help others. People in our study felt most engaged when they were doing something meaningful with a clear impact on a real human being.

CHANGE RESILIENCE CHALLENGE #6

Engagement is less about what we get and more about what we give. How can you make a difference in a customer's life right now?

An organization that provides its employees with the tools to make a real impact on people's lives is the company that will have the most engaged employees. When employees say they receive the support to deliver exceptional customer experiences, what they are really saying is:

"I can make an impact."

"I own the issue."

"There are people who need me."

"I am not helpless."

"I am in control."

"I can perform to the highest (exceptional) level."

This surprising finding was reinforced by the fact that employees who interacted directly with customers demonstrated a higher level of engagement than their colleagues (48% compared to 37%).

When working with a client in the automotive industry, we saw this problem first-hand. Technicians were consistently the least-engaged group in the entire organization. The nature of their work requires them to focus on fixing cars, which leaves minimal time for face-to-face interaction with customers.

While the technicians felt that they needed more support and tools, we suspected the lack of customer contact was the real issue. At first, the dealership's owners opposed the idea of allowing the technicians to speak to or meet with customers. The owners believed it would disrupt the process, and that only service advisors should speak to customers.

But they agreed to a pilot program to test the idea: once a week each technician would join the 5pm service drive – their role would be simply to thank customers for the opportunity to service their cars.

This simple act delivered amazing results. The technicians felt appreciated. For the first time, they were able to see the gratitude in the eyes of the customers. Allowing them to speak to customers gave their work greater meaning and provided them with a sense of empowerment. It helped them realize that they were not moving metal, they were moving people.

Their work was valuable.

Engagement Driver #1: Give people the power to have an impact on someone else's life.

Not long ago, I reviewed a training manual for a logistics company. In the 137-page document, the word *customer* appeared only seven times. The topic of the correct angle at which to hold the keys as a driver picked up a package, however, was thoroughly discussed and documented.

It was evident from the manual what mattered to the company: process. Employees were not encouraged to deliver exceptional customer experiences (unless, of course, if it had to do with holding their keys at the designated angle!).

When an employee is trained at that level of granularity to submit and accept, he will not have any room left for change resilience – or for the customer. The customer was referred to as a *recipient* or a *shipper* but not treated as a human being with needs. Employees were referred to as an integral part of the process, but were expected to behave in a predictable one-size-fits-all way.

Only when employees feel that they are empowered to do what is right will they feel engaged. The company defined its employees as process operators and never bothered to show them how their work made a difference. It failed to contextualize the work and robbed the employees of understanding the impact of their work.

A much better approach would be to introduce even the technicians to their customers and their customers' expectations early on.

Engagement Driver #2: Put customers at the centre and empower people to serve them.

True or false: If managers are engaged, then their employees will be too.

False. While 53% of managers and supervisors demonstrated engagement, only 40% of nonmanagers did. The management-employee engagement gap was even more striking when we compared the engagement level across different management ranks. Some 69% of the C-suite demonstrated engagement compared to 47% of employees.

While our study conducted in conjunction with the *Harvard Business Review*, revealed that communication is an issue between senior executives and employees, it is not the only issue. There is a real disconnect when it comes to ownership. In most cases, senior leadership creates change programs and dictates strategies around change. Employees are just expected to jump on board.

Employee ownership = engagement.

Passive attitudes and a victim mentality =
low engagement and poor performance.

We recommend a fundamentally different approach: one that puts employees in the driver's seat. We train them to face the facts just as their CEO would, enabling them to make their own decisions and own the outcome. (I'll explain this technique in detail in Part Two of the book.)

Engagement Driver #3: Give employees personal ownership of the strategy.

If you're a manager and you want engaged employees, you need to give each and every employee ownership over the strategy, as well as the tools, training and authority to execute it. You also need to give every employee – even the technicians – ample face time with customers.

How Can My Work Benefit Others?

Combine these three key drivers, and a clear picture emerges. Whether you're being asked to embrace some new change at work or you're willingly embarking on a personal transformation, the same drivers apply. If you want the change to stick, ask yourself how it could benefit others.

We all have the opportunity to start viewing change as a liberating tool that frees us to evolve and upgrade our value to customers, to become a trusted advisor, to elevate our interactions so that each one has a real impact on customers' lives. Yes, helping an entrepreneur fill out the forms necessary to take out a small-business loan is important, especially if he doesn't know how to do it himself – however, helping him plan the growth of his business and offering advice is priceless.

This is why understanding your core cause is so important. The impact you make is as unique to you as your smile – it's a way of expressing your real personality and how much you care.

Change can be liberating. It can free you up to take your performance to a totally new level you never believed possible. It allows you to engage with the human aspect of your work and add a personal and authentic touch. But there is a choice involved – you must choose to become the better version of yourself. You must choose to be a force of good in the world.

PART TWO

four

ARE YOU FUTURE READY?

We Crave Hope in Times of Change

In one of the most iconic superhero scenes of the past several decades, Spider-Man battles Dr. Octopus on a racing New York City subway train. Seconds before the train flies off its tracks into the water below, Spider-Man uses all his strength to slow it down and eventually stop it.

(Is there any better metaphor for our fear of change coming at us fast and furious?)

But you don't need to have seen that particular film to know about the allure of superheroes. They're the subject of four of the world's ten highest-grossing movies. Together, those four films – *The Avengers*, *Avengers: Age of Ultron*, *The Dark Knight* and *The Dark Knight Rises* – earned over $2 billion.

Between DC Comics' Superman, Batman and Wonder Woman and Marvel's Hulk, Thor and Captain America, we are flooded with stories about superhumans willing and able to save the world from the evils threatening our very existence. Despite the never-ending parade of sequels, America hasn't gotten sick of them.

While the weapons may have gotten bigger and the bad guys badder, someone watching *Man of Steel* in 2013 probably shared the same sentiment as someone reading Superman comics 75 years ago: they're both fascinated by the superhero who chose to use his gifts not for fame and fortune, but rather to save the world.

The phone booth might be obsolete by now, but I am confident Superman has found a solution to his personal transformation. After all, the world isn't going to wait for him. The villains are all around us and crime never sleeps. But that's okay – superheroes transcend time and place. They provide the same solace to fans today as they did when they were first introduced to the world so many years ago.

While many of the most popular superheroes' powers remain the same – think the Hulk's strength, Thor's hammer and the Man of Steel's laser eyes – they are nimble enough to adapt to the newest threat and restore peace and order in a matter of a few fight scenes.

What is the attraction? Why are superheroes still as relevant today as they were nearly a century ago? What is it about them that has us so obsessed?

This has been debated by many researchers and culture experts. One thing is clear: superheroes don't just provide the fictional citizens of Gotham City, Metropolis and Smallville with a sense of stability in an ever-changing world – they give it to us, too. In a world that is changing at warp speed, we naturally latch on to the characters that don't. Who else but a superhero can render change unimportant? Superhero stories assure us that, at the end of the day, peace will be restored.

Everything will be okay.

In addition to the sense of confidence in law and world order, superheroes deliver one more promise. In the comic series and book *Superman: Birthright* (2003–2004), we finally learn the meaning of the *S* on Superman's chest.

"The symbol of the House of El means hope," Superman's father, Jor-El, tells him. "Embodied within that hope is the fundamental belief of the potential of every person to be a force for good. That's what you can bring them."

In times of turbulence and unrest, superheroes give us hope that better times will come.

Their stories are also inspiring – some people watch these movies and want to *be* a superhero, not just buy the T-shirt. These films teach us to believe in our own powers and to embrace change, not fight it. Superheroes, simply put, are the better versions of ourselves. The more proactive and motivated versions. The versions that demonstrate a higher capacity for change resilience. The versions of us that can and will engage with change on behalf of the world.

On the surface, our love of superheroes seems positive enough – but is there something deeper at work? Does our obsession tell a story of an unwillingness to adapt to the increasing change we face all around us? In other words, are we taking comfort in knowing someone else will make all the bad go away?

After all, in a world full of superheroes, we don't have to rush to change.

Which brings us back to you. What will your reaction to change be? Will you wait around for a superhero to save you, or will you become one?

To ask the question another way:

Are you future ready?

By that, I mean: Are you ready to embrace the unknown? To be proactive and stay ahead of the game? To own your destiny – and use your skills to help others? To be a force for good in the world, not just buy the T-shirt?

Our five-step Future Ready Impact process was designed to help you get there – and to take your colleagues and your organizations with you. We'll be diving deep into these steps in the chapters that follow, but here's an idea of what's to come.

Step 1: **Face it!**

The first step in embracing change is getting honest with yourself about the reason for it: anything from industry trends and technology advancements to a changing customer base or environmental factors. Your challenge? Face the change squarely and objectively and decide your next step.

Step 2: **Analyse it!**

You're not a robot. It's human nature to fear change. This is what Step 2 is all about: understanding the emotions associated with change. You're going to explore the pain, the fear, the lack of readiness and any other emotions standing between you and the rational facts you faced in Step 1. You'll learn to recognize them, understand them and ultimately move beyond them.

Remember, you're *supposed* to be afraid of change. What separates the change resilient from the rest of us is that they've developed a strategy to move past that fear.

In this chapter, you'll learn to join their ranks.

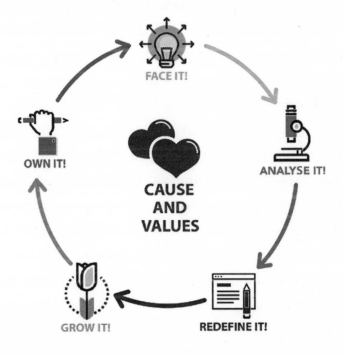

Step 3: Redefine it!

At this point you have a good understanding of both the rational reasons for change and your irrational opposition to it. It's time to reframe the change and understand how it helps you fulfil your purpose. By focusing on your core cause and understanding how the proposed change is in alignment with that, you can create a hopeful future you can love and embrace. Change will become something you want to pursue as a means to fulfil your hopes and dreams.

Step 4: Grow it!

It's not enough to just imagine a beautiful future. Step 4 is all about training for it and creating a safe space for you to start embracing new behaviours and develop your confidence around the change without fear of public embarrassment.

Step 5: Own it!

At this point, change is yours. You are ready to bring the change into your daily practices and behaviour and put your own spin on it. Not only will you be better able to roll with the new changes, you'll be better equipped to see the next change on the horizon.

Whether you're facing a personal change or a professional transformation, these five steps are designed to accelerate change and guide you to the next place you belong. They will empower you to be the authority of your life. So let me ask you: are you ready to change?

It's okay. You don't have to be quite yet.

Just trust that you'll get there – maybe even faster than you think.

five

FACE IT!

I was once asked to give a workshop on customer experience to the IT department of an industrial company. The executive team wanted to make sure the session was a success, so rather than use a regular meeting room, they rented a hotel ballroom. Employees were told they'd be attending a workshop with a specialist in customer experience who would be discussing how they could add value and elevate their game.

When I began to speak, one employee raised his hand and said, "Sir, would you just give us our package and let us go? We don't really need the big speech."

"What do you mean, your package?" I asked.

"We all know that you're here to fire us," he said. "Just give us our packages and let us go home."

"What made you think that we're here to fire you?"

"Why else would the company book a hotel and hire consultants?"

"No, you're not fired," I said. "We're here to talk about how to delight customers!"

It was one of the most surreal moments I've ever experienced. But it really drove home how much fear people live with – the fear of constant change, the anxiety that their company was just waiting for them to drop the ball. It wasn't just one person, it was the whole department. They were all sure their work was about to be outsourced. They'd given up.

Welcome to the world of irrational fear we're all living in.

Thanks to the explosion of popular behavioural economics books such as *Freakonomics* that have swept the market in the past decade, we've learned one key lesson: people are too human to act logically. Many of those books reference the groundbreaking work of two Israeli-American psychologists, Amos Tversky and economics Nobel Prize recipient Daniel Kahneman. Their research established that we all have biases that transform the truth into our own comforting version of reality, one in which we avoid taking action at all costs and view change as dangerous and destabilizing.

Let's be honest with ourselves. The majority of us do not raise our hands when a new project or change is proposed. We sit quietly looking around to see who will volunteer first. We are scared of failure. We are comfortable being followers. Why take a risk?

Instead of facing the truth, we invest time in denying it – or at least, ignoring it. It's a natural human reaction. Embracing the truth takes energy. So we sit and adopt the 'you first' approach. It worked for us so many times. Why stop now?

In this chapter we will take the first step away from such passive reactions to change. We will start owning it – fast.

Inertia Is Not a Strategy

When Chobani Greek yogurt was introduced in the United States by a Turkish immigrant named Hamdi Ulukaya, the big yogurt players like Dannon and Yoplait treated it as a niche product – possibly a fad, definitely something they didn't need to pay attention to. Their well-established market presence, robust advertising budgets and proven customer loyalty seemed to reassure them of a successful future. A small blip on the radar surely couldn't disrupt their ongoing success, could it?

Think again.

What started out as a small 4% market share niche in 2008 has grown exponentially over the years. Now that the big players have been forced to join the movement, in 2015 Greek yogurt accounted for 50% of the yogurt market.

Now, Greek yogurt is not a new phenomenon. In fact, it has existed for centuries in Greece and Turkey – and the global yogurt brands were well aware of it. So why did the yogurt industry giants ignore Chobani? They spend millions of dollars each and every year tracking market trends and forecasting customer needs, tastes, aspirations and emotions – and yet they missed this one?

Greek yogurt was not some secret recipe someone whipped up in their garage – and Chobani obviously had some early fans. The issue was not a lack of information.

The big players simply ignored the information they didn't want to believe.

When you take into account the natural human bias against change, our approach to data and emerging trends is predictable. We try to fit new information into a reality that's comfortable to us or dismiss it as invalid. Regardless of how powerful and representative the data we're presented with, if it's telling us to make a change, we tend to ignore it.

It's Time to Take a Look in the Mirror

Why do I suggest starting the process of embracing change by facing the facts? Because if we cannot agree on the change we need to make – and the impact it will have on both our personal and professional lives – we will not be able to move forward and transform.

Facing the facts is difficult. Therefore we wear different lenses when we face any data suggesting that change is needed. These lenses come in many different colours. None of them, unfortunately, are the ones we need: the colourless lenses that allow us to see clearly through to the mirror.

+ The blue lenses tell us the change is doomed from the start. Why bother changing? It won't help.

+ The red lenses make us mad. The data must be wrong – it certainly contradicts what we believe to be true.

+ Pink lenses see the status quo as rose-colored, diminishing the intensity of the data and the sense of urgency. "I'm working on it already," we tell ourselves with a smile. "It's all good."

+ The green lenses tell us change is too expensive. Staying the current course is the prudent financial approach.

+ The black lenses simply will not see anything. We know our job so well that we don't have to pay attention to industry news and trends. Just keep doing the same work and everything will be fine.

Do you remember the Wells Fargo fake accounts fiasco of 2016? Employees at the bank created millions of fake accounts for real customers in order to boost their sales figures and make more money. This disaster resulted in the firing of 5,300 employees and eventually led to the resignation of the company's longtime CEO on October 12, 2016.

A case of denial on an astronomical scale. How could so many people see the facts and not address them? How could so many people believe they would get away with this? Did they really believe they would never be caught? What were they planning to tell their customers about the fees they were charging for fake accounts?

We are not dealing with one rogue person here. This was an institutional approach. Their aggressive sales quotas – the green lenses – biased the judgment of 5,300 employees who were able to put their integrity aside and even risk their jobs to increase profits.

While this example may seem like an outlier, we've all been guilty of denying the truth at one time or another. For many people, our preoccupation with the here-and-now is enough to keep us oblivious to the inevitable change happening all around us.

CHANGE RESILIENCE CHALLENGE #7

Facing the facts requires you to be proactive. Set aside a regular time to take note of industry and global trends. What opportunities should you be seizing?

They used to say that when a New York City taxi driver gives you a stock tip, it's too late. Let's not wait for a cabbie, the media or

Aunt Susan to inform us of the emerging trends. Let's face the facts early on so we can treat them as an opportunity – not an inevitability.

Your Preconceived Notions

Experience, it's said, is the best teacher. As we go through life, we experience successes and failures and develop opinions about what works and what doesn't. The problem with this bit of advice is that our knowledge can lead to avoiding new experiences. As we gain more wisdom, we try fewer new things. Our change muscle does not get toned, it gets neglected.

While we should respect our life experience, we need to re-member that sometimes the lessons we've accumulated can slow us down – like blinders hiding from us what's in plain sight. What others see as obvious may not even register on our radar.

When we first encounter the Next, we ought to suspend those preconceived notions. The same notions that probably led to Nokia ignoring the smartphone while Apple was developing it. The same notions that led many on Wall Street to ignore the signs of a loom-ing financial crisis.

Personally, I cannot imagine myself sleeping in someone else's home. The few times I've stayed with family members have been hor-ror stories – each time I longed for a comfortable hotel room instead. I would much rather avoid all the unexpected surprises and invasions of privacy. Yet for me to ignore Airbnb and the massive, disruptive change it's inflicted on the world of hospitality would be a big mistake.

The life lessons we carry with us can help us avoid mistakes and minimize pain, but they should not block our progress. We should be very conscious of those preconceived notions and open our eyes to the world of possibilities around us.

Stop Playing the Victim

Lisa was irritated. Her boss was asking her to start using a new mobile platform. She resented the new social platform of the company and blamed the CEO for not understanding the business. They'd gotten by for decades without apps, and she saw no reason why they should change what had worked. Lisa felt personally attacked – as if she were the only one being asked to adapt to a new technological reality. But Facebook and Twitter are happening to everyone – the CEO, the company's customers – not just her.

The next time you feel the urge to blame management (or Mark Zuckerberg) for foisting some new tool, technology or task upon you, remember that the people who ask us to change are often responding to trends that were forced on them as well. They too need the courage to face the truth and take action before it's too late.

When your leaders are struggling to understand and chart the right response to changes that are bigger than they are, the last thing they need is an attitude of "What are you doing to *me*?"

When my colleagues and I looked closely at the victim mentality we were seeing so much of, we noticed an interesting phenomenon. Employees would argue vehemently that management was wrong.

That whatever change was being suggested was the wrong move for the company to make.

But then when we'd ask them for an alternative, more often than not they would point to the status quo. They'd have no well-thought-out alternative. Most, in fact, had been ignoring altogether the shifting circumstances that management was trying to deal with. In other words, they were leaping right into rejection mode without attempting to understand the big picture.

A victim mentality delays the inevitable, but will not help you avoid change forever. The sooner you recognize you are playing the victim, the faster you will be able to start dealing with reality in a mature, responsible way.

What Would a New CEO Do?

That's the question Andy Grove, the legendary founder of Intel, would ask at critical strategic junctures: "What would a new CEO do?" In his book *Only the Paranoid Survive*, he describes how this little game would help him look at problems with a fresh set of eyes – and without worrying about politics. He wanted to face the facts squarely and without any personal biases.

We can take a cue from Grove whether we're driving a change initiative, being asked to embrace a new tool or system or approaching a change in our personal lives.

If you're a manager, put your employees in the CEO's seat. Let them face the same facts you've been given and reach their own conclusions. It is amazing what happens when instead of forcing employees to be passive recipients of change, you ask them to join you in analysing harsh realities. Many initiatives fail because leaders don't take this step, giving employees a perfect excuse not to change. By putting employees in the driver's seat, on the other hand, you allow them to engage with the facts and reach their own conclusions.

As for those of you who've been asked to change or who are proactively diving into the Next, try imagining the advice you would give to someone seeking the same results. Pretend you have no emotional entanglement. As you consider the complexity of the problem before you, you will start to see a clear direction for the future. You will start to sense the urgency – and understand why a change is necessary.

I always find it fascinating how this little game creates such tremendous insight that previously didn't exist...

Or did it? Was it really the exercise that led to the new insights? I suspect not. In many cases, people already knew the change had to be made, either consciously or subconsciously. The real power of this game is that it gives people a new perspective and sense of urgency. It shows employees that leadership respects their viewpoints. It gives everyone an opportunity to take ownership of the situation and act as mature adults in the process.

LOYAL OR DEPENDENT?

Lea, a branch manager of a major bank, had been resisting adapting to digital channels. She just didn't feel her customers needed this tool. After all, they were loyal. If they'd wanted digital banking, they'd have left long ago.

But were customers loyal – or dependent?

This was a tough question for Bank Manager Lea to answer – after all, she'd been seeing the same customers for years. They clearly wanted the services the bank offered – otherwise, why were they coming back?

But what about New CEO Lea?

She could see that by not giving customers an option to try digital banking, the bank was forcing customers to use methods that were becoming increasingly dated. Why? Because she and her colleagues were afraid to discover they might be wrong.

By giving customers the choice between digital and traditional banking, Lea's branch could discover what customers really wanted – and ensure ongoing customer loyalty.

The CEO Seat exercise was a huge *Aha!* moment for Lea. She'd never considered that her actions were creating unwanted dependency. Because of her resistance to change, she was taking her customers for granted – and in the process, creating a dependency they would eventually resent. It was only when she sat in a more distant, objective seat that she could see the truth.

Put yourself in the New CEO's seat.

Now it's time for you to put yourself in the New CEO's seat. When you assume this role, remember to assume a broad, multilensed perspective by evaluating the following four dimensions: operational excellence, customer relevance, operational relevance, and market relevance. As you evaluate each dimension, ask yourself: What do those trends mean to our current performance? And how will they affect future performance?

		Operational Excellence *Customer Complaints*		Customer Relevance *Customer Trends*	
		Current Performance	Future Performance	Current Performance	Future Performance
IMPLICATIONS	Strategy				
	Products				
	Processes				
	Behaviours				
	Customer Engagement				
	Employee Engagement				

+ **Customer complaints:** What's the gap between your desired outcome and the reality? Your customer complaints are a big clue. (If you're embarking on a more personal transformation, consider feedback from family or friends about the habit you're trying to kick or adopt.)

+ **Customer trends:** What do your customers want now — and what will they want in the future? Staying on top of those trends will help you stay relevant.

+ **Technology trends:** Are you paying attention to the technologies your customers and competitors are using today?

What technologies are disrupting other industries — and might they have an effect on yours? Are you looking for new opportunities to create and deliver solutions to customers?

✦ **Competitive trends:** You don't exist in a vacuum. Your competitors are also pursing their own strategies — and in the process reshaping the marketplace. Pay attention to their behaviour.

Operational Relevance *Technology Trends*		**Market Relevance** *Competitor Trends*	
Current Performance	Future Performance	Current Performance	Future Performance

This exercise isn't just about *understanding* how trends and technology will affect your performance, relevance or behaviour — it's about *making decisions* like a CEO. It's about realizing the complexity that top executives deal with and drawing relevant conclusions that will ensure ongoing health, growth and prosperity.

Each and every one of these dimensions may have a direct impact on the way you formulate your strategy and engage with your colleagues and customers. They also should guide your future performance — although they will never give you the answer. That is your decision to make.

Remember, there is no substitute for a courageous, objective look at reality. Which means – there is no substitute for YOU taking a direct look at reality.

Emotional Denial

An insurance company recently embarked on a huge transformation. Prior to launch, the team running the change program conducted a detailed reality check similar to the New CEO seat exercise, but on a far larger scale. All the signs indicated they were on track. Senior management was fully invested.

And so they launched with complete support and commitment... only to watch commitment start to erode almost immediately.

Why?

"We're like an alcoholic who checked himself into rehab," one of the executives reflected, "but deep down hopes that his counselor will buy him another drink."

There is so much truth in that single statement. The facts were hitting them straight between the eyes. They agreed with the reality check. They agreed with all the facts. They were committed rationally, but were in denial emotionally.

But there's a good reason for that.

Face it! is the first step on this journey – but far from the last one. The insurance company was courageous enough to face the truth, but not ready to handle their deep denial. That is what the next chapter, *Analyse It!*, is all about.

six

ANALYSE IT!

I don't know about you, but each time I step on the scale, I face the truth. And I hate it. I gained weight by ignoring what I ate and neglecting to exercise more. The facts are staring at me in neon. But knowing the truth doesn't really mobilize me to take the right action. (In fact, I often take the wrong action – by reaching for the closest comfort food I can find.)

While I asked you to suspend your fears and emotions during *Step 1: Face it!*, I will now ask you to turn them loose. Without understanding how your emotions are holding you back from changing, you cannot successfully move forward.

A rational decision alone will not turn you into a champion for change. Your mind will still resist change, and the closer you get to it, the more aggressive the resistance will become. (How do I know? Because if this weren't the case, you wouldn't need this book.)

This phase is arguably the most difficult. Few of us want to admit that our 'soft', emotional brains are refusing to ignore the hard facts. No leadership team wants to accept that their well-researched, promising strategy is subject to employees' emotions. "It's business, not personal," they want to scream.

But the reality is very different. Our emotions often make the choice about whether innovative strategies are adopted or not. Emotions matter. They are the bloodline of change.

Traditional approaches to change begin by asking: "What would *enable* success?" We, instead, ask: "What *stops* people from embracing change?"

This means taking our focus off the future and placing it on the past.

More often than not, our previous experiences with seemingly similar changes cloud our ability to see a proposed change clearly. Which means: presenting a beautiful vision of the future will not by itself make us more open to change.

Before developing new skills, we must develop emotional readiness.

Many people find this approach to change challenging. Maybe we've been putting off a change for a while, and we fear that if we don't jump in fully, the change won't stick. Or perhaps we're driving a change initiative and want our team on board ASAP.

If you're feeling that urgency, take note: our experience has shown that a failure to address the emotional aspect of change often leads to delays. The new behaviours are short-term and impact is incremental. The plan or program will not deliver the desired results.

At this point in the process of adopting a new strategy or process, you or your team should have reviewed the facts and gotten clarity about the implications of changing or staying the same. Yet you're still probably grappling with some creative and persuasive arguments. Let's see if you recognize any of the following excuses:

+ **"No way! This is stupid. It'll never work."** This 'best defense is a good offense' approach seeks to confront the change head-on with complete denial. If you're calling an idea stupid, are you *really* giving it a chance? Probably not.

+ **"If people really wanted it, they would have told us."** This is one of my favourite excuses, the 'blame it on the customer' approach. If customers didn't tell us about it, then it must be a bad idea.

My challenge to anyone with this excuse: Are you *really* listening to customers? Maybe customers *are* telling you they want it. But that's not the only problem with this excuse: if you wait for the customers to tell you something, you're also waiting for them to tell your competitors.

+ **"This change doesn't affect me."** I get where you're going with this one. The change is not relevant to me, my industry, my department, my region, my you-name-it. This classic "I agree, but ... " excuse is a deflection of responsibility. When you make this argument, you're basically saying that you operate in a different reality than the one everyone else is living in – that you're not affected by the same changes as everyone else. Not only is it delusional, it's dangerous. Do you really want to be the last one on board?

+ **"Not now, it's not the right time."** Another "yes, but" deflection, this time focusing on timing rather than roles. Yes, this is the right approach moving forward (wait for it ...) but the timing is wrong. Give me a little more time (how about a decade?).

+ **"We tried it and it didn't work."** What did you try? Why did it fail? Was it the idea or the execution? Did you have the tools, skills and attitude to succeed? And just because your first attempt failed, does that mean the idea is bad or the change is unnecessary?

+ **"I don't have the money/It's not in the budget."** How lame. Let's blame the finance department or our own lack of funds. Such an easy target! Of course, you or your company

have yet to budget for this change – many
budgets only take into account current operations. The real question is: what don't you
want to take off your budget?

Sound too real? That's because these are the universal reactions
of people responding emotionally to change. These arguments are
often a thin veneer hiding deeper anxieties. Instead of denying
that, let's really understand what's happening. Let's explore the real
fears hiding behind the excuses and use what we discover to get
future ready.

When it comes to change, the heart often leads the mind. So
how can we win over our hearts? To answer that question, I'll share
two scenarios where the superficial rejection of a change was hiding
a deeper emotional fear.

FEAR OF GETTING HURT

When designing a cancer treatment centre experience, it's important to consider every aspect – everything from the look of the
waiting room to the amenities available in each treatment room.
But you can design the most comfortable and soothing centre in
the world, and if the employees are not engaged, patients will feel
no comfort.

When the subject of emotional engagement came up with
nurses at the cancer treatment centre we'd been asked to design, I
was surprised to discover their reluctance to truly engage with patients. While they knew quite well the importance of connecting

emotionally, they worked to maintain boundaries with patients whenever possible.

When we asked them about it, they explained it was a method of self-preservation. The pain their patients experienced – and the fact that some didn't make it – was incredibly difficult for the nurses. As a result, they were not willing to open up. They were afraid to get hurt.

As one nurse put it so succinctly, "I do not want to go to any more funerals."

As we examined the issue further, we realized that many of them saw their patients' suffering and deaths as a sign of the nurses' inability to connect with them. Despite all their efforts, many patients didn't get better.

Thanks to that deep emotional insight, we decided upon an approach that addressed the nurses' frustration and sense of helplessness. We began to design the patient experience as a journey, not as a destination, redefining the role of the nurse as a personal guide. No longer did nurses need to feel responsibility for 'solving' the patient's illness. Instead they could act as the patient's companion.

By recognizing the nurses' distress and sense of impotence, we developed a new approach to managing change. The results were phenomenal. The nurses felt a new sense of purpose and fulfilment. The patients' reaction to this authentic care was beyond our wildest expectations. Some even got tattoos of the logo of the cancer treatment centre in appreciation.

Change may be painful, but there's no use ignoring it. Addressing the root of the pain and fear often helps you come up with the right solution for everyone.

HIDING BEHIND HUMOUR

Have you ever cracked jokes about your own or your organization's inability to change? Adopted a 'been there, done that, this too shall pass' attitude?

Cynics may hide behind humour, but make no mistake: cynicism is not funny. It kills hopes and dreams and prevents others from creating and imagining. On the surface, cynics may seem cool and disaffected, but don't let them fool you. Cynicism often hides a great deal of emotion. At the heart of cynicism is the lack of willingness and stamina to get up and do something different.

Many cynics are former hopefuls who experienced disappointment and simply gave up. Now they cannot muster any more strength to rouse themselves to attempt something different. Why? Not because they are exhausted.

No matter what they say, they still care. (If they stopped caring, they would have moved on long ago.) But they are lost. They have lost connection to the core cause that would make the effort worth it. Cynicism is their condolence song, a desperate grasp at the past all the while knowing deep down it is not going to last.

It's time to call cynicism what it is: a force destructive of imagination, creation and a better future. Cynics are crying for help. So it's time to give them what they're asking for: a regular reconnection with their core cause.

=== *CHANGE RESILIENCE CHALLENGE #8* ===

The next time you catch yourself cracking a joke or rolling your eyes about a change you're attempting, take note. Is your humour or blasé attitude really an attempt to hide a deeper fear about your inability to change?

There Are No Miracles

Here's a little test. Read the following (100% real!) statements and take a guess at what company people are talking about:

+ "[They] have tried big, transformational efforts before, but most failed because the culture killed them."

+ "You had operations pushback, security and fraud pushback, creative pushback. There was never any shortage of pushback."

+ "There was land-grabbing, finger-pointing, and, quite frankly, a lot of yelling in closed-door meetings."

+ "[A] culture that is all smiles and happiness, and everyone is going to give you a hug. But you have no idea who is working against you. You come out bruised and bloody."

✦ "Let's put it crudely: people were protecting their jobs."

You've probably run through the list of dysfunctional companies: Wells Fargo? Enron? Think again: these statements all refer to one of America's most beloved companies, Disney.

In 2015, *Fast Company* published a cover story about Disney's attempt to incorporate electronic passes called MagicBands into its parks and hotels. The quotes illustrate that even for an organization as well versed in change as Disney, change is painful.

When I read the article, I was shocked. I am used to seeing these sentiments in more established, less agile organizations. I thought that in organizations like Disney, this type of raw emotion and back-stabbing would not take place. It was a rude awakening for me.

Why is change so painful? Why aren't there magic solutions? Because change is not about miracles. It is about people – people who are struggling with their emotions and fears. And no matter how brilliant a new idea is, if you focus on the idea and not on the people, you will end up with lukewarm results at best.

As shocking as this story is, it also reminds us that resistance to change is a fundamentally human quality. No person or organization, no matter how fun or inspiring they appear on the outside, is immune. It reminds me that we're all in this together – so if you're ashamed about your emotions regarding change, you can let those feelings go.

Accept that change is going to be uncomfortable, and dive in anyway – now, that's bravery.

Creating the New Predictability

For many of us, predictability and consistency are critical to success. People crave predictability because it gives us a sense of control in the world (a false sense, but a sense, nevertheless). And organizations that need to report quarterly results to demanding investors must build a rigorous discipline around predictable performance.

In the name of predictability, we develop routines – and document them. A predictable world is a world we can control. A world with no risk.

We do not want risk – only reward.

We do not want chaos – only clarity.

When change is looming, we immediately cling to the beautiful, predictable, safe world we've built for ourselves. It is the reason that many organizations, even when facing the most obvious change, will try to minimize or delay its implementation by creating pilot programs or going into overanalysis mode to 'best understand the implications'. Can you imagine a diabetes patient saying, "I will test insulin two days a month and see what happens"? Of course not.

Some sense of predictability will be sacrificed. Some risk will be assumed. It's the reality of change – you cannot predict exactly what will happen once you start making changes. The good news is, change gives you a chance to rewrite the future. Wouldn't you prefer to live in a future you created than one someone else forced upon you?

Let's look at how one company triumphantly managed this step.

The Courage to Go Beyond

For years, a UK-based gas company had suffered from poor customer relations. Actually, that's putting it mildly: When employees went to install new gas tanks at customer sites, at least once a month one of them was likely to return with a black eye. Once, customers even staged an attack on the company's headquarters, destroying company property.

When the company had a meeting to discuss the analysis of the cause of customer anger, their managing director, Lisa, stood up and said, "We are going to fix this. There are no other alternatives. If you have a problem with it, you are fired. There is the door."

You can imagine the silence in the room.

It was a difficult meeting – but the company was focused. Lisa gave them an option: If they were afraid, they didn't need to be part of the changes the company was about to make. She, too, was scared. But it was time to go beyond fear.

Prior to the meeting, the company had a Net Promoter Score (a management tool measuring customer loyalty) of negative 31. In other words, every time they interacted with 100 customers, they created 31 more unhappy customers.

Twelve months later, the score was a positive 54.

What happened?

The facts Lisa presented initially were painful. But her willingness to confront and not deny them was an important step forward. Her approach ultimately shook her team out of their fears and challenged them to take action. Yes, she made it clear that rejecting the change wasn't an option, but she also provided the support, consulting, tools and resources necessary to usher in the change.

I attribute their success ultimately to Lisa's moment of courage. It was scary and unpleasant, but there comes a time when we need to conquer our fears and take action. She did just that.

How prepared are you for the change ahead?

Our emotions influence and often blind our view of change and what we need to do about it. Those emotions will not disappear on their own. The more we understand them, the better the chances of addressing them and progressing beyond them.

Before I introduce the five types of change resistance, it's time to find out how emotionally prepared you feel about the change you're facing. Rank the following statements on a scale of 1 to 5, where 1 means you strongly disagree and 5 means you strongly agree.

- ✦ I stand to lose very little from the proposed change.

- ✦ I see a bright future for myself if I make the proposed change.

- ✦ I have the skills and/or resources to adapt to the proposed change.

- ✦ I am likely to succeed when it comes to implementing the proposed change.

✦ I am ready to publicly communicate my commitment
   to the proposed change.

✦ I see how the proposed change aligns with my past work.

✦ I have the time to adapt to the proposed change.

✦ I am empowered to adapt to the proposed change.

✦ I can easily let go of my old behaviours.

✦ I will feel more empowered if I adopt the proposed change.

Add up the scores for your answers. Now let's see where you stand:

✦ **The Fighter (score of 10 to 19).** Your change
   resilience is essentially nonexistent. You fear
   change with a capital *F*. Your thinking is deeply
   rooted in the past. It's time to challenge the 'glory
   days' narrative in your head.

✦ **The Cynic (score of 20 to 29).** The change is
   definitely bringing up some fears. You see some
   hope in the future, but not necessarily in *this*
   future. While you may not fight change proactively, you will happily share your negative
   thoughts with others. You hope things will settle
   down without impacting you. You simply don't
   understand why all this has to happen. To adapt,
   you'll need to focus on all the ways change will
   make your life easier.

+ **The Observer (score of 30 to 39).** You're a bit curious. You're willing to let your guard down in order to consider the possibilities. While you aren't convinced, you're willing to learn more. You will form your opinion only once you're convinced either way. To increase your change resilience, try learning as much as you can about both the risks and the rewards of change.

+ **The Optimist (score of 40 to 49).** You demonstrate healthy change resilience. You aren't blind to the possible downsides, but your belief in the promise and possibility of change more than compensates for that. Deep down, you *want* change to work. You bring a positive attitude to the conversation. There are still some issues to iron out, of course, such as learning new skills and gathering resources. To adapt, direct your attention to the tools and techniques necessary for proficiency in the new ways.

+ **The Accelerator (score of 50).** You are enthusiastic and unstoppable. You *are* the change you want to see in the world. You demonstrate an abundance of change resilience and serve as inspiration and encouragement to your peers. You belong in a mentoring position, helping others embrace change faster. To succeed, you need everyone else on board so you can all function as a team. To make the most of your skills, step into a leadership role and help others on the journey.

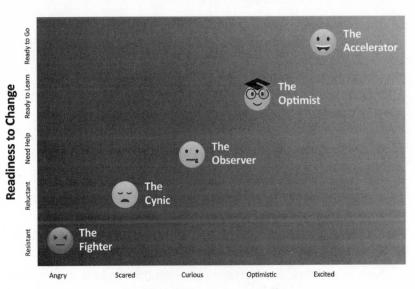

Emotional Engagement to Change

This exercise measures two attributes that affect our change resilience: *readiness* and *perception*. Readiness is your capacity to execute on change — it's all about learning and practising new tools and procedures, gaining confidence in new ways of working and learning to appreciate them. Readiness is willingness and confidence combined. Perception, on the other hand, is all about beliefs and convictions. Some of us are driven by the narrative first and adapt to tools later.

To build change resilience, we need to work on the heart (the narrative) and the hand (the practices). We need to develop a convincing story about the future, and we also need practical tools and support to get there — practices we'll be exploring in the next two chapters.

Now that you have more understanding of how change resilient you are, ask yourself the following questions:

- ✦ What am I really afraid of?

- ✦ What will be the impact on my future if I let fear dictate my actions?

- ✦ Whom can I voice my fears to?

- ✦ How can I conquer that fear?

There are no real guarantees and assurances when it comes to adapting to change. But since we are already discussing fears, let's introduce one more: FOMO – the fear of missing out. FOMO is a term that has gained popularity in recent years, especially on social media. Often, millennials use it to describe the feelings they have when they're staying in on a Friday night while everyone else is going out.

But when it comes to exciting new changes in our world, a little bit of FOMO can actually drive us to overcome our fears and embrace change. If our doctor recommends a new treatment regime for managing a chronic disease, skipping it would mean giving up on our future, on everything from seeing new places to experiencing our children's growth. Ignoring the latest technologies may prevent us from communicating more effectively with our loved ones. Just try to convince your grandchild to speak on the phone. Good luck with that!

Every change brings with it a new promise, a promise we will most definitely miss if we do not adapt in a timely manner. You could miss out on a life experience or an opportunity to make an impact on the world.

Is your fear worth missing out on something so important?

seven

REDEFINE IT!

If you're waiting for transformation to happen to you, I have some bad news: you're going to be waiting a long time.

Transformation requires action.

Here's the thing: change is going to happen whether you like it or not. But when change happens *to* you, it becomes your weakness, not your strength. Your goal should be to lead change, not be led by it.

At this point, you've gotten clear about the reasons you need to make a change and you've analysed the fears that might be holding you back from jumping on board. Now it's time to accelerate your commitment to change.

Acknowledging our fears does not mean we should let them dictate our future. In this phase we will bridge the gap between past and future. We will personalize the change and understand the role it plays in our life's journey. This phase enables us to view change as a continuation of – not a departure from – the past.

No One Needs You

Why do you need a car? Probably to serve your transportation needs. You need to get to work, drive your children to school and, of course, travel. For all this, you need four wheels, an engine and other basic parts – and as long as they're all working, the car serves its purpose of getting you from point A to point B. Most cars on the market today will satisfy these basic needs.

Why do you need a luxury car? This is a very different question. If the hundreds of models of cars on the market will serve our basic transportation needs, then why would someone pay four to ten times more for a car? The answer is, most people won't.

That was the challenge Mercedes-Benz USA faced when it set out to reinvent its customer experience.

Karl Benz, the founder of the company and the inventor of the first car engine, established the company's motto: "The best or nothing." As Mercedes-Benz grew, it struggled to maintain the best customer experience in the marketplace and relied heavily on the quality of its luxury vehicles. But competitors like Lexus, BMW, Audi and Volvo quickly caught up and matched some of Mercedes-Benz's capabilities.

As we were working on redesigning the customer experience and creating a consistent standard of excellence across 360 dealerships and 25,000 employees, we knew we needed to redefine the company's narrative. Our biggest insight was: "No one needs a Mercedes-Benz!" When we shared our revelation with the company's executives, they gave us a look that could only be described as, "Are you *trying* to lose this project – or have you lost *your minds*?"

"No one needs a Mercedes-Benz," we insisted. "They *desire* it. You are not in the needs business. You are in the dreams business. You ought to redefine your business narrative to start connecting with customers' dreams, not their basic transportation needs."

This new story helped employees appreciate that, while car models and new features come and go, none of those things define who they are. The cars are merely a vehicle (no pun intended) for customers to achieve a higher goal – in this case, a dream. By assuming the role of dream-maker, employees were inspired by the emotional impact they would have on customers. They no longer saw themselves as purveyors of utilitarian tools of transportation. They realized they played a meaningful role in the customer's life.

One afternoon during our time working with Mercedes-Benz, a customer showed up at one of the dealerships and asked to sit in a car. It was a rather strange request. The customer explained that he was terminally ill and had wanted to drive a Mercedes his whole life. He just wanted to live his dream for a few minutes. The employee who received the request was already empowered in his new role as a dream-maker and arranged for a top-of-the-line S-Class for the customer to test-drive. He knew quite well that the customer was never going to purchase the vehicle.

It didn't matter. He was no longer a salesperson. He was a dream-maker.

This redefinition empowered Mercedes-Benz employees to re-calibrate their mission. Thanks to their willingness to transform, they achieved, for the first time, the number-one position in customer satisfaction according to J.D. Power and Associates, ending Lexus's 20-year run.

Redefining your mission and connection to customers can help you absorb and adapt to change. While working with Mercedes-Benz, I came across a number of people who had been in the business of selling cars for 30 years. One of them told me that he had been selling cars since 1968! Imagine how many behaviours these individuals had to uproot to allow room for new practices and methods.

But the process of defining their purpose helped them challenge their old assumptions and embrace a new operational road map.

Who Do You Work For?

One of the most fascinating aspects of my work is watching people develop the confidence to take initiative. Their behaviour often surpasses our wildest expectations and reaffirms our foundational belief that many people have the capacity to change hidden within them. All we need to do is remove the obstacles and accelerate their takeoff.

After attending a session focused on teaching front-line employees to think like their customers, John, a product manager, decided to take action. He approached his colleagues, more than 200 of them, and asked them a simple question: "Who do you work for?"

John asked each colleague to write his or her answer on a piece of paper and hand it to him. They all complied without thinking too much of it. After all, the answer was clear. After a few hours the news of this exercise spread, and more employees sought John out to contribute their answers. Once the results were in, John compiled the responses and read them aloud, one by one, to his colleagues.

"I work for Joe, my direct supervisor," was one answer.

"I work for my regional general manager," was another.

"I work for the CEO of the company," stated another employee.

"We all work for the shareholders of the company," said someone else.

The list went on:

"I work for my paycheck."

"We all work for sales."

"I work to finance my family's lifestyle. My wife and my kids are my bosses."

While there were some outliers and wisecrackers, for the most part the answers were consistent. Employees worked for management: the people who hired them, the managers they reported to, the ones who could fire them.

After reading all the answers, John shared the following insight:

"One day, your direct supervisor will retire. You don't work for him. One day, the CEO will get another job elsewhere and leave you behind. You don't work for him. One day, the head of sales will win the lottery and move to Jamaica without as much as a backward glance. You don't work for him either. One day the shareholders will sell their stock and move their investments elsewhere. You don't work for them either. We all have one ultimate boss. It's our customer."

John continued: "If your supervisor doesn't show up to work, you still have a job. If the CEO is on vacation, you still have a job. If the head of sales is promoted and moves elsewhere, you still have a job. But if your customers stop showing up, you have no job. We all work for them. They are our one and only boss."

I was in awe when I heard about John's actions. His method was as profound as it was simple. The clarity of his message cut through all the corporate politics and bureaucracies. He knew who he worked for and knew what his core cause was.

We often forget this simple yet invincible truth. No customer = no business = no job. It is as simple as that. If customers stop entering your store or visiting your website, the game is over.

Recognizing this is a critical step toward discovering your cause. You may not directly interact with customers every day in your line of work, but somewhere down the line there is a customer who needs you. Every job, every transaction has a customer. That person needs you to deliver to the best of your ability. The only way you will do so is if you recognize how much that customer needs you.

How can you connect their need to your cause?

Who Does Your Work Impact?

Your boss or your colleagues might be the reason you come to work every day. If so, I am truly happy for you. Not too many people love their work environment or the people they work with. However, as our nationwide study revealed, liking your boss does not equal engagement. It may sustain you in your role for a while, but in the long term, if you don't understand the impact you're making on customers' lives, that joy will fade.

It's easy to be confused about whom you really serve. Your direct supervisor gives you goals and assignments. Your finance department controls the budget and gives you targets. Your CEO sets the company's vision. All of those internally focused goals and assignments may lead you to forget the simple reality: at the end of the day, there is an external customer living with the consequences of your work.

In other words, you make an impact on someone you might not even meet. Your work either directly or indirectly provides a solution to some problem they're having. When you think about the people who benefit from your activities and performance, remember that they're human beings – with hopes, dreams and fears that might be very similar to your own.

In her work as a professor at Case Western Reserve specializing in elderly care, Eva Kahana conducted a 20-year study of a 1,000 elderly people to learn what leads to higher satisfaction in life. The life of the elderly is full of change – from loss of loved ones to chronic diseases and loss of capacities. These changes are very personal and meaningful.

Kahana's research discovered that those elderly people who volunteered experienced a higher level of satisfaction with life despite the painful changes they'd had to endure. Living a life of impact helped them cope with their own personal changes – and it may have helped them stay alive longer and live more meaningful lives.

Understand Your Impact

Try to remember a moment when someone expressed gratitude for your work and the impact it made. Bring yourself back to that moment and remember how it made you feel. This moment is representative of you living up to your highest potential. Connecting with it can help you understand the impact you can have on people. If you're still unsure about the impact you have on customers' lives, ask yourself:

- ✦ Who are my customers?

- ✦ Why do they need my solution?

- ✦ How do they feel not having my solution?

- ✦ How does not having the solution affect their personal lives? Their professional lives?

- ✦ How does not having the solution affect their dreams for the future?

- ✦ How does not having the solution affect their relationships with their loved ones?

- ✦ What fear does my solution help them overcome?

- ✦ What excitement would my solution create for them?

- ✦ What would my solution empower them to accomplish?

- ✦ What time would it give them?

- ✦ After acquiring my solution, how would they use it?

- ✦ Whom would they share it with?

- ✦ How would they brag about having it?

Understand My Customers ➡	Identify Impact of My Solution ➡	Recognize the Emotional Impact
My Customers' Dreams	Customers Use My Solution to Solve	The Emotional Impact My Solution Has on My Customers
My Customers' Fears	Elevate	
My Customers' Aspirations	Empower	
My Customers' Pain Points	Engage	
My Customers' Unmet Needs	Using My Solutions, My Customers Feel...	

When you sell a new technology solution to an IT person, you are not just selling a replacement for an outdated system. You are providing job security. You're helping someone provide for their family. You're boosting their self-esteem by allowing them to stay relevant in the ever-evolving world of technology.

Of course, you may never hear that directly. All you heard was a question about the bits and bytes. But in reality, you are not in the technology business. You are in the job security and self-confidence business. You are in the happy-home business.

That's your impact.

On an organizational level, your new technology may allow a company to stay competitive and deliver better value to its customers. The impact you have may include saving the jobs of employees who would otherwise be subject to downsizing.

Keep in mind that the impact you make is different from the solution you deliver. The solution is the transaction. The impact is what you make people feel and do. We measure solutions and impact differently. Transactions are always measured in operational numbers such as cost and time. Impact is measured in human influence and lives affected. This explains why few people find it fulfilling simply to finish a project on time and on budget. It feels far more amazing when a customer says, "Thank you!" We want to feel powerful, to believe we can improve people's lives and make things happen.

Serving Internal Customers

Some people only serve internal customers – their colleagues, managers, those who report directly to them. As a result, it might be a bit difficult to see the power they have to make an impact. But every activity can make a difference in someone else's life.

If you submit an inaccurate and incomplete expense report, guess what? Suzy from the accounting department will now have to live with the consequences. She may end up having to chase you to get everything documented correctly, which means it will take her twice the time to complete the job. As a result, she might miss her evening spin class or her daughter's piano recital, or she might not have time to watch her favourite show that evening.

Even seemingly menial tasks have an impact. Deliver less-than-exceptional work, and someone will suffer the consequences.

═══ *CHANGE RESILIENCE CHALLENGE #9* ═══

Change doesn't affect just us. It can also have an impact on our colleagues and customers, and even on our family and friends. Ask yourself: how can this change support my commitment to everyone in my life?

Impact Performance versus Technical Proficiency

Every time we think about the impact of our work, we move beyond mere technical proficiency and into 'impact performance'.

People and organizations committed to impact performance share two interesting characteristics:

- ✦ They talk about what a privilege it is to serve people. They view their work as a series of opportunities to help others. Not everyone was invited to do this important work, but they were, and they're grateful for that.

- ✦ They hold themselves to a higher standard. They do not hide behind excuses when someone questions their behaviour, or quote official procedure when the customer is unhappy. They do whatever it takes to get the job done for their customer. If processes

or manuals support their goal of making an
impact in their customers' lives, they will use
them religiously. If official rules don't work in
a particular situation, they will find a creative
way to accomplish the desired results.

Compare that behaviour with companies that see processes and manuals as a goal – organizations where rules play a primary role and customers are treated as one-size-fits-all. Those that aren't interested in impact performance often have low change resilience. Instead of adapting to others, they expect everyone to adapt to their rigid systems.

Those who embrace the impact they can make, on the other hand, demonstrate high change resilience. They are willing to change to fit the unique needs of different situations or customers. After all, they consider it an opportunity to serve the needs of others – and if they have to think creatively to make an impact, bring it on.

Rock versus Water

Through the work I've done, I've noticed that people use different analogies to represent the change process. One manager described it as a "12-round match" – he saw a long battle, with every step representing another punch to the gut.

The problem with analogies is that they set our minds and, eventually, our behaviours accordingly. If I view change as a wrestling match, I will go into it with the preconceived notion that it is going to hurt. You better believe that will affect my mood and readiness to manage change.

As we shift from the old notion of 'Change everything' to 'Evolve while staying true to your core cause', we also need to change the image of change in our minds.

I've also heard change referred to as an "impenetrable, rigid, stubborn rock" to be scaled, as if moving on with our lives meant somehow bypassing change. In this analogy, change is a huge obstacle to overcome. On the other side of it is our destination.

In fact, true transformation is more like water than like a rock. It requires fluidity and constant movement. Otherwise, it will stand still and become toxic. Here's another thing to remember about water – and about change: they both find their way through the cracks of stubborn rocks, wearing away at the stone over time.

As we redefine what change means to us, we should redefine the images we associate with it. It is time to replace the old stubborn rock with constantly moving, flowing, fresh water.

What's your core cause?

It's time to identify your core cause and assess how it's connected to the change you're facing. The following two exercises will help you achieve this goal. You may have to complete the first exercise only once, because once you've defined your cause, it may not change significantly in the future. The alignment exercise that follows, however, should be applied regularly when preparing for a new change in your life.

Exercise 1: Choose your cause.

Imagine that you are free of any financial worries or obligations and have the opportunity to volunteer with the charity of your choice:

+ Which charity would you choose? An organization dedicated to healthcare reform? A mentoring program for kids? An environmental protection group?

+ Why would you choose to volunteer there? Is it because you're attracted to manual labour, specialized work or fundraising?

+ How would you feel while volunteering there?

+ What would you be known for at the charity? Would you be the comic relief, the one who always sees the silver lining, the person who wears his heart on his sleeve, the strategic thinker or the most dependable volunteer?

Exercise 2: Define your mission.

Now use your answers from the previous questions to identify your mission. The previous exercise should focus your thinking and allow you to assess yourself in the most pure, unbiased, unrestricted way.

+ What do you love? (Your mission)

+ Whom would you love to help? (Your world)

+ How would you like to impact them? (Your skills and values)

+ What future do you want to create for them? (Your hope)

The answers to the above questions should allow you to answer the following questions:

1. What values define you?

2. How would you like to make an impact on the world?

MISSION-CHANGE ALIGNMENT

Now that you know your cause, you are ready to redefine any change you face so that it aligns with who you are.

Understanding how this change will affect the lives of your stakeholders and what your desired impact is will help you view change as a friend and not a foe. If the answers aren't clear the first time, repeat this exercise as many times as needed. Let the questions sink in and allow your mind to explore new ways to create the impact you desire.

Discovering how many people really need you and the power you have to help them overcome their fears and realize their dreams and aspirations should be exciting. It will allow you to view and redefine yourself from a position of strength. It will help you create a new, more powerful version of yourself – one that can, despite any limitations, improve other people's lives.

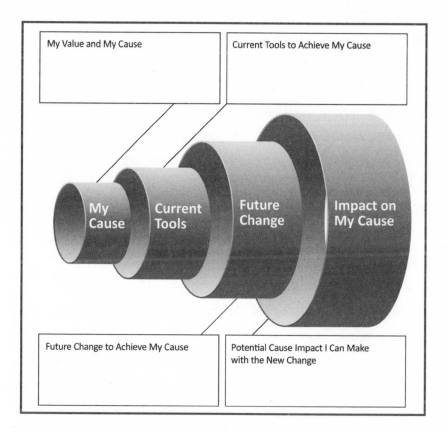

| My Value and My Cause | Current Tools to Achieve My Cause |

| My Cause | Current Tools | Future Change | Impact on My Cause |

| Future Change to Achieve My Cause | Potential Cause Impact I Can Make with the New Change |

Personalize Your Impact

As you work on discovering your core cause, it is imperative that you personalize and internalize it. This is especially important when a change reflects the broader cause of your organization. Yes, of course you want to be in alignment with the transformation, but you also want to make it your own.

One technique for making your cause deeply personal is to give it a name – redefining your role based on your impact, not just your technical performance. There's research that makes the case for this technique. A May 2016 article in the *Harvard Business Review* described a London Business School study by Professor Dan Cable. Cable challenged employees at a hospital chain to give themselves new titles that described what they do. An infectious disease specialist became a 'germ slayer', for example. Cable then compared the engagement of those employees who'd adopted creative names to a control group with more typical titles. The newly titled employees demonstrated "lower levels of emotional exhaustion, felt more validated and better recognized for their work, and experienced a greater psychological safety, which can promote free information exchanges."

Most formal titles reduce people to a set of tasks and rob them of the ability to take pride in what they do. Jobs that remind us of the impact we have on others elevate our performance in a way that makes a difference to us – and everyone we affect. Here are some of the names people we've worked with have created for themselves. A receptionist who staffs the front desk and answers the phone named herself the Director of Customer First Impressions. A nurse no longer just administers treatments; she's the Patient Spirit Lifter. I've met a salesperson who called himself the Awe-Inspirer, a customer service rep who designated herself the Red Carpet Roller, and a call-centre employee who elevated her title to the Queen of Everlasting Customer Love.

I don't know about you, but I know that if the Queen were to call me, I would pay attention.

Other people adopted titles like Customer Dreams Fulfilment Manager and Director of Customer Excitement. Once, I even met a Director of Customer Happy Endings. (Keep your thoughts PG-13, please.) In each instance, a title described a person's *impact*, instead of the tools or techniques they used to achieve that impact. What often starts as a bit of an awkward exercise becomes an inspiring, personal self-discovery.

Now it's your turn. How would you elevate your formal, technical-description title to one that describes the impact you create?

Name your impact.

1. Describe the emotional impact your work has on the people you serve. Do not focus on what you do for them, but rather on how they *feel* about your work.

2. Lace a word such as *people, colleagues, customer* or *employee* (in the case of managers) into the title to ensure you are focused on the right impact.

Yes, at first glance, the titles you come up with might feel a little silly. But you don't have to share them with anyone. What's important is your commitment to your emotionally engaging title and your role as an impact-maker. In my experience, this approach has inspired many to see their performance from a completely different perspective.

If you feel comfortable doing so, share your title with some of the people you work with or whose lives you have an impact on and see if they agree. Use your impact-maker title as a source of inspiration, and let it set your standards for the experience you create for others.

While the names you come up with will vary, they are all some variation on Customer Delight Creator. To do your job well, you must ask: "What is delight?" This question will help centre your mind on your cause and remind you of the true impact you can create every day.

Making the Choice for Cause

The good news is: your cause already exists. People need you. Your customers are the true beneficiaries of the exceptional work you do (not your boss, your CEO or the faceless shareholders of your company). Deliver real impact, and you will not need to wait for your annual performance evaluation to know about it. The reaction will be immediate. Customers will thank you personally, comment on your Facebook page, retweet your message and recommend you to others. Or simply smile back at you.

Defining yourself as an impact-maker means facing people directly and never hiding behind excuses or organizational bureaucracy. It's about owning a problem and sticking with it all the way to the solution. Performing that way is a personal choice – and it's not a onetime choice. You have to choose to make a difference in people's lives and decide to do so every day. You need to take the lead and not relent until you've delighted the people you're serving.

It will not be easy. Some situations may be very challenging. Some customers may seem unrealistic and overly demanding. But we can't replace them, and we should not try to convince them that they need anything less than the best. By committing to the cause, we are committing to making a difference in their lives the way they need it.

Now, of course, I am not advocating for you to do anything that you believe will harm your customers. If they are uninformed or desperate and are seeking the wrong solution, making an impact could involve educating them and empowering them to make smarter decisions.

At a physicians' panel, I was asked about the trend of patient empowerment; often people will ask their doctors for tests or medicines that are not in their best interest. Some physicians told me that they have given up and stopped arguing with the patients.

"If it doesn't hurt them, I will let them have it, even though it will have little to no real impact," one physician said.

But impact performance is not about blind submission to the customer's wishes. There are times when you can have the most impact by saying, "No, it's not good for you." This can happen when a patient demands unnecessary treatments, or when a small-business owner attempts to take out too large a loan. Real impact means doing what is right for the people you work with or for. That is why this way of working is so powerful and meaningful.

We all work for people. Anywhere there is a need, there is a *person* in need – be it a citizen applying for a passport, a guest in a hotel, a homeless person at a shelter, a donor at a performing arts centre or a buyer of a hamburger. They are all customers of our products, services and solutions.

But first and foremost, they are human beings with dreams and needs.

It's time to start seeing the people you serve as your North Star, as the cause that makes it all worth it, as the reason to exist and thrive and raise the bar for your personal standards. Make it a personal choice to live your life and conduct your work that's aligned with your cause.

Working with people is a privilege. It may not feel that way at times when the demands are high or the challenge is hard. But in the end, we are getting the chance to have a real impact in the world. We are never helpless.

We always have the power to make a difference.

WE WANT OUR CAPE BACK

What happens when you work in a mission-based organization, but you've lost connection to your core cause? This happened to employees at a nonprofit dedicated to serving people with depression and other mental illnesses. Thanks to an unmanageable workload, employees were feeling stressed and underappreciated, and saw little opportunity for career growth. After we heard about their many pains, we asked them to write a letter to the CEO.

Now, usually when we give teams this exercise, the letter summarizes the issues that we talked about. To our surprise, this letter to the CEO was completely different.

It said: "Everything we do is so important, and you're such a hard worker and you're doing so much for everyone."

What the heck was going on here? The level of denial was overwhelming – partly because the organization had such a strong core cause. Who wanted to admit they were unhappy doing such important work?

When the CEO asked me for feedback, I told him: "Your employees want their cape back. They joined this organization because they believed in a mission. When they tell you they are being underappreciated, what they're saying is not necessarily 'I need more money'. What they are saying is: 'I need my cape back. I want to feel that what I'm doing here is meaningful. I want to be reminded that I'm great'."

Ongoing Transformation

So once you've defined your core cause, you have built the bridge over whatever change might be flowing your way, right?

Yes and no.

It is true that your core cause does not change and, as a result, can serve as a compass to help you navigate uncharted waters. But just as having a goal does not make it a reality, having a core cause is just the beginning. You need to work on it every day to bring it to life. Otherwise, it's like throwing a penny in a wishing well.

Different transformations will present new opportunities to be relevant and evolve. Each time you set out to change something in your organization or your life, you'll need to see how it aligns with your core cause. Only then can you approach change from a point of strength – and understand the larger role it plays in your journey.

eight

GROW IT!

I hope that by now you can see change for what it is – inspirational. However, this insight is not guaranteed to last. There are two more steps to building lasting change resilience. Without them, the threat of defaulting to old behaviours is ever-present.

Now it's time to build your confidence in your ability to work or live the change effortlessly. After all, we want to make sure we are flawlessly delivering on our promise. To achieve this, we need to grow our skill sets. Welcome to *Step 4: Grow it!* During this step we will operationalize the cause that inspires us and apply it to our everyday activities, behaviours and interactions with customers.

Operationalizing an idea means bringing it to life, making it real and relevant. In other words, this chapter is all about shifting from ideation to activation. While our cause can stay high-level, lofty and conceptual, we must make it real through our actions, communications and behaviours. This is how we fulfil promises.

Without this crucial step, great insights die on the vine.

But I'm not ready to fully embrace this change! you might be thinking – and for good reason! No one is expecting you to fly out of a phone booth with an *S* on your chest quite yet. Change needs to be properly scaled – so we're going to start small by practising our new behaviours in low-risk ways.

Start Small and Safe

Some people and organizations take the leap rather quickly from inspiration to impact. However, in our experience, it's wise to first create a safe environment where you or your employees can experiment and increase your confidence – and your chance of success.

Let's face it, few of us want to try something new for the first time in front of a judgmental audience. Even the most experienced actor must rehearse his lines, the emotions behind the words and his chemistry with his fellow actors. Just because the actor is experienced does not make him qualified to perform without preparation.

So why do we assume that practice isn't important in other scenarios?

We all need time to practise in a safe environment to develop our confidence and commitment. No one wants to test some new technique in front of their customers or supervisors, because the chance of failure and embarrassment is significant. We need to make it possible for our colleagues – and for ourselves – to try new things, fail and learn from our mistakes in a way that does not penalize us.

Walk in Your Customer's Shoes

To make an impact, you first need to understand your customer. But this is not always easy. If you love music and you serve people who love music, you can relate. But the cardiologist who's never had a heart attack will never be able to fully understand what his patients are experiencing. A fireman who has never had a fire almost instantly erase the history and the memories and everything that he held dear will never truly understand a survivor's sense of loss after a fire.

In the case of luxury product sales, the gap between the socio-economic backgrounds of the employees serving the customer and the customers themselves is quite significant. These two groups come from different backgrounds and live very different lifestyles. When we began working with a Canadian luxury brand that was losing market share to its competitors, the gap was evident. Not only could the employees not relate to their customers, they resented their customers for being so demanding and having such high expectations.

So we devised an assignment to help them better understand their customers.

The goal of the exercise was clear: you need to walk in your customer's shoes. The execution was a bit unusual. Sixty employees of the company were sent on a discovery mission to understand their affluent customers more thoroughly. To accomplish this task, they were each given money to visit and shop at luxury boutique stores such as Prada, Hermès, Louis Vuitton and Montblanc. To top their experience, they were instructed to dine at some of the star-studded restaurants of Toronto. (You are probably feigning sympathy for them for the tough assignment, but mind you, they were working.)

In preparation for the assignment, they were taught how to be a critic for the day and judge the quality of the experience they were receiving. While shopping and dining, they were experiencing the lifestyle that their customers were accustomed to, and they took note of how they were treated, what language was used during their conversations, and how complaints were managed. The dining experience heightened the learning, as they saw multiple employees working seamlessly to delight the customer. The stores and restaurants were not aware of the program and were paid normally for their products and services. (All products purchased were donated to charity.)

The lessons the participants learned from this exercise were phenomenal. The impact far exceeded any other method we'd used in the past to help employees understand the customer perspective. While traditional methods included reviewing focus-group results, customer videos and customer surveys, none managed to drive the message home like giving employees the personal experience of their customers. Their senses were heightened and they learned to appreciate the demanding expectations when top price is paid for a product or service.

To their surprise, not all of the high-end vendors they visited performed well. Some luxury store employees 'profiled' the customers based on how they were dressed or how they spoke, and treated some of our exercise participants poorly, assuming they were there only to browse. In one case, a luxury store employee followed the customer around the store, walking behind him and folding everything he touched, making him feel very uncomfortable. Some store employees made comments on the shoppers' low budget and made them feel inferior.

During the dining experience, special requests were sometimes frowned on, as the restaurants wanted to honor the 'chef's vision', making the diners feel unwelcome. In other cases, our participants were welcomed with a cup of espresso at a luxury store, making them feel like a million bucks. Small touches made the employees feel valued and important.

Thanks to this personal, hands-on experience, our client's employees were challenged to apply what they learned to their day-to-day interactions with customers. Every transaction was redesigned to delight the customer.

The final outcome exceeded all expectations. By personally walking in their customers' shoes – even if only for a few hours – employees were able to appreciate the impact their work makes on their customers. Two days later they left with a brand-new blueprint for success that recognized the need to elevate their performance and pay attention to every customer during every interaction.

The *Grow it!* step is critical to making change stick. Often, learning and flexing our new muscles in a safe environment can give us the confidence to make it happen. This 'walking in our customers' shoes' assignment created new insights and drove new commitment to accelerate the change. It made it personal and, therefore, easy to execute.

Later in this chapter, I'll guide you through the process of walking in your customer's shoes. But first, let's understand why this kind of customer-centric approach to change is so successful.

Activating Your Cause

I once came across a story of a mortgage loan officer who found out that a customer he was working with was not going to proceed with a loan. During the home inspection, the customer had found a number of issues he determined were too expensive to fix. The customer, who was a US veteran, was left to sleep in his car. The loan officer took it upon himself to fix the issues in the house and prepare it for closing. He even took pictures of the renovations he'd made as evidence to get the mortgage approved.

What a wonderful example of someone who lives by his cause. The loan officer refused to be a mere paper-pusher. He could easily have refused the loan and simply abided by the bank's rules. But that was not who he was. He was not the process guy. The process was merely a tool. He was committed to helping his customer fulfil his dream of owning a home. And because the process didn't work, he elevated his commitment and did whatever was necessary to fulfil his cause.

What would it take for you to step so confidently into your new role?

Many of the programs we teach focus on becoming customer-centric: learning to understand your customer and adapting your performance to meet and exceed their expectations. Rationally, participants get the message. They too believe in exceptional service and commitment to excellence. Where they get stuck is not on the concept, but on the execution. I frequently hear: "Okay, so how do I do it?" or "Tell me what to do. I think I'm already doing it, but I'm obviously not doing it well enough."

Where to begin?

I love the story about the mortgage loan officer because he seemed to know instinctively how to move beyond process and live by his cause. Operationalizing your commitment to change isn't just about adding in a new task here or there. Rather, it's about examining how you spend each day and determining where the new change will have an impact and how it will alter the way you perform. The outcome should be the same, if not better. The way to get there was just upgraded.

The beauty of our customer-centric approach is that, over time, you'll be able to adapt on the fly – just like the loan officer – letting your core cause guide your every interaction. But what many people don't realize is that you can actually 'rehearse' for that kind of exceptional service.

Here's the process we recommend:

1. Map your daily activities and responsibilities.

   + What are you in charge of?

   + How are you being measured?

   + How do you fulfil your responsibilities?

   + List all of your activities and the customers who benefit from them.

2. Identify the impact a change will have on your daily operations and activities.

   + How will the change impact your activities?

   + What will you have to do differently?

   + What will stay the same?

   + What might be eliminated altogether?

   + What will the impact be on time available to you?

3. Visualize your new activities with the change.

   ✦ What will a typical day look like for you?

   ✦ How will it make you feel?

   ✦ How will it impact your customer?

   ✦ What does it do to the time available?

   ✦ What tools would you need to execute it?

   ✦ Draw a clear image of the newly delivered activities.

4. Create a step-by-step diagram of the new ideal state.

   ✦ What skills do you need to master?

   ✦ What behaviours should you adapt?

   ✦ What behaviours should you stop?

5. Develop a communication plan. One of the best ways to adapt to change is to develop means and methods to communicate it to others. Imagine you are communicating the change to your customers.

◆ How will you explain the need for it?

◆ How will you communicate the customer's role?

◆ How will you explain your future role?

◆ What will be your choice of words?

	(1) List of Activities	(2) Current Impact of Activities on Customers	(3) What Can You Change?	(4) How Does the Change Impact Your Activities?
Daily				
Weekly				
Monthly				
Quarterly				
Yearly				

(5) New Skills	New Tools	New Behaviours	Behaviours to Stop

Let's look at a banker whose goal is to start operationalizing her job as the Creator of Customer Financial Security. Yes, the change she's grappling with is her bank's use of a new digital platform. But that doesn't change her role as someone whose job is to help customers feel like their financial lives are safe and secure. We can actually rehearse how she can deliver the same exceptional service using a new set of tools:

A customer arrives to discuss her unexpected divorce. Her husband has always managed their finances and she is now left with no clue as to how to move forward. Her life as she knows it is in ruins, she's an emotional wreck and now her financial world is in an equally dismal state.

What does she need right now?

Let's walk through the Future Ready Impact process to see how a banker would be ready for this situation.

First, the banker will need to *Face it!* – get honest about the reason for the change. In this case, the change is a new digital platform that customers are demanding. Then she'll *Analyse it!* – get crystal clear about any fear she might have about the change. Next, she'll *Redefine it!* – understand how the change aligns with her core cause.

The old banker would have responded that the customer needs a line of credit, a new credit card, maybe a new checking account – all of which the customer can apply for via the new digital channels. But the banker in touch with her core cause will recognize that the customer's real need is for clarity and support. She needs to regain control over her life. She needs to develop new financial understanding. Without an emotional readiness and a sense of control, no financial product is going to make a difference. What she needs right now is a sense of hope and reassurance that the loss and sense of destruction she feels in this moment will not last.

The cynic in this situation might say that she should find a friend. Maybe. But that friend still won't be able to support her financial path going forward. An empathetic banker would be far more suitable to help the woman in this situation.

Thanks to digital platforms that can perform a lot of the banker's old tasks, she is liberated to spend more time providing comfort and understanding to this particular customer. She can guide the customer's next steps, helping her see which products will best suit her needs. Helping the customer create a budget and enlisting her in digital alerts that will enable her to manage her budget correctly will create the sense of control – and hope – that she currently lacks.

By fusing the power of digital tools and human empathy, the banker can create a lasting memory and a value her customer will not forget. At the end of the day, in her moment of truth, she was there for someone who needed her.

Elevate Your Value

As new technologies infiltrate our lives, we need to be fluid not only when it comes to adopting new tools, but also when it comes to elevating our service offerings. This has become very clear to anyone working in the automotive industry – not to mention most car owners. Technologies that just a few years ago were an exclusive privilege in luxury cars are now widely available in every vehicle.

Working with Mercedes-Benz, I was amazed when a technology that was originally created for the flagship S-Class became available in the lower C-Class vehicles in a matter of only two or three years. This expanded availability, of course, forced Mercedes-Benz to continually reinvent the high-end S-Class to distinguish it from the rest of the fleet.

By the same token, in many industries, what was considered added value just five years ago is now common practice.

In other words, we need to elevate our standards. In the past, customers received all their information from salespeople. Today, customers often know more than salespeople due to the availability of information on the internet. Salespeople must evolve – or they face extinction.

In the past, every complaint or customer issue had to be handled by customer service. Today's customers are solving more and more problems via self-service tools in apps, online sites and kiosks.

In the past, we needed an airline employee to issue a boarding pass ...

In the past ...

In the past ...

In the ...

You get the picture.

As more and more services become automated, the challenge for us all is to reconsider the human role in our industries. Every time a new opportunity is created, an old source of value dies. Knowledge of a product is no longer enough – a sales associate now needs to provide emotional support. Customer service is no longer about answers; it is now about empathy. Travel is no longer about finding a cheaper price, but rather about celebrating a meaningful moment in a special destination.

And your role, whatever it is, will continue to evolve and grow as technologies and change eliminate yesterday's value.

What If?

Let's explore how the opportunities that accompany a change will enhance your ability to fulfil your core cause. How will the change help you accelerate fulfilment, expand reach, and deepen impact?

Every change opens new doors. When we focus on the past, we blind ourselves to the new opportunities that accompany change. When we focus on our core cause and the customer impact we deliver, on the other hand, we can see the new world of opportunities that change ushers in.

We need to explore these new opportunities with 'What if?' questions that challenge the way we do things.

We need to explore the 'What's next?' that will be exceptional.

We should avoid at all costs replacing one status quo with another.

After all, if we do not explore possibilities to inspire our customers, someone else will. So if we are already going through the disruption that comes with change, why not aim higher and go for exceptional?

+ If adopting a new technology means you'll have less paperwork, what would you do with the newly discovered time?

+ If you don't have to teach the customers the basics, what meaningful conversations could you have instead?

✦ How could you evolve your role and
impact if the bureaucratic aspect of your
work was eliminated?

Operationalizing the Change

It's time to turn intentions into actions. In this step, we will review
the work you've done so far, converting the knowledge and commitment you've generated into an actionable practice. We are now
taking the conceptual and making it operational.

Step I: *Understand your impact by walking in your customer's shoes.*

✦ Define your customer impact, the outcome
and emotions you create for your customers.
How do you make your customers feel?
What needs do you fulfil for them?

✦ Define your role from the customer's perspective. Create a new job title that describes
the impact you make. (For example, a sales
associate's new title might be Customer
Dream-Maker.)

✦ Identify daily tasks. List the daily tasks you
carry out to create customer impact.

+ Align the new change with your daily tasks. Identify new ways to get the daily tasks completed utilizing the change.

+ Elevate your value. Identify the new value you can provide in the context of the change and your interactions with your customers. What can you do for the customer that you couldn't do before? How would you save the customer time, money, etc.?

+ Look for more opportunities to make an impact. Identify new services or capabilities you can introduce to the customer that you could not offer before.

Step 2: *Flex your change resilience muscle with 'growth playing'.*

Now it's time to flex your change resilience muscle by assessing how the change will affect your routines and practices. Try practising 'offstage' before you go live with your customers or those who are impacted by the change.

Some people hate the idea of role playing, so I have to remind them this is not simply a tool for actors and other performers. Even the best doctors must rehearse. If you still find yourself turned off by the idea, consider replacing the term *role play* with *growth play*. Because, in fact, we're not simply rehearsing a role, we're growing. This is not about perfecting, this is about building some confidence. This work is about practising upward, not practising horizontally.

Practising will allow you to develop your confidence and help you prepare answers to any questions that may arise after you've made a change. You may wish to ask a friend to play a customer, or you can run through scenarios on your own. Develop three detailed scenarios that include customer comments, demands and emotions. For someone working in customer service, they might include:

+ Customer onboarding

+ Customer complaint

+ Customer special request

Now play out each scenario with the change incorporated. This will help you develop your confidence around doing things the new way. Make sure to anticipate any questions the customer might have and prepare answers. The purpose is to make sure you are ready for prime time.

You can use the same process for a change in your personal life. Develop three detailed scenarios for whomever the change will affect: your parents, spouse or friends. How can you live your change boldly and confidently?

Something fascinating happens whenever people participate in this exercise: it's incredibly cathartic. People often create a new character that incorporates the extreme behaviours of many of their customers.

While it's certainly fun to play 'bad customer', I think there's something deeper at work here. Some of the most challenging moments in our lives occur when working with customers and trying to develop trust. This exercise gives us an outlet for our frustration so that we can bring our best selves to our customers.

One flight attendant who tried this technique enjoyed playing an obnoxious platinum loyalty customer with a crying baby, a laptop and an unquenchable thirst for free liquor. While this was an extreme example of a person she was unlikely to ever meet, I learned all about the new challenges of working with airline customers: the absence of patience and a lack of appreciation for how long certain things take to do.

Customers today seem to forget that there are other passengers on board, the attendants explained. All manners seem to have vanished – a simple "thank you" or "please" seems to be a precious commodity, they added.

So I asked them, "What is the one thing every customer wants?"

"An upgrade," they answered.

Then I asked them a question that puzzled them.

"How many passengers do you serve every month?" I asked.

With an average of 200 passengers aboard every flight and 25 flights per month, that is 5,000 passengers served each and every month. That is 60,000 passengers a year!

"Every passenger has a dream they wish to fulfil," I explained. "Every passenger is pursuing something by traveling somewhere. And you have the privilege to be part of that journey. You might not be able to solve all their problems. And yes, there are always going to be those few irate passengers. But let's focus on the majority, the ones we do have the power to impact. We may not have a seat in first class to upgrade them to, but we can give them an 'emotional upgrade'."

An emotional upgrade can take many different forms: an honest interest in the customer's well-being, a sincere compliment on her dress, or a simple yet heartfelt smile. An authentic approach that brightens someone's day is worth far more than an automatic smile in first class.

CHANGE RESILIENCE CHALLENGE #10

An 'emotional upgrade' is a superpower you can access in almost any situation. Providing a sincere emotional uplift to the people you engage with can make every situation a tad more manageable. How can you activate this superpower today?

The more we practise authentic engagement, the more powerful and joyful we will feel. Now it's time to unleash the power we have and bring change to life. It is time to own the change and make it ours. To move from practice to action.

nine

OWN IT!

We are at the final step of a long journey of self-discovery. Not only did you confront the truth of the need for change, you courageously recognized your emotional resistance to it. You explored how the change can help you better achieve your core cause. You developed new confidence around change, then explored how to incorporate change into your daily routine.

Now it's time to really own it.

To own change, you need more than just determination. You need a plan with goals and milestones. You need to celebrate successes and create a process for learning and adapting to whatever new changes come your way.

Remember, change is not a one-time event.

An Ecosystem of Success

Many people have a vision of success but have no plan to operation-alize it. Others have the opposite problem: they take all the right steps but fail to recognize success when it arrives. They simply let it pass by without any sense of jubilation and accomplishment.

To be change resilient, we must address both issues. How? By developing an 'ecosystem of success' – a set of activities that will allow you to activate new behaviours and weave them into your life. In this chapter, you'll learn how to:

+ Define and visualize success

+ Create visual reminders

+ Develop daily rituals

+ Capture the success stories

+ Experiment every day

+ Add aspirational challenges

+ Solicit feedback

+ Create a milestones journey

+ Plan to fail

+ Celebrate achievements

Living Your Cause Through Change

- Visualize Success
- Visual Reminders
- Daily Rituals
- Success Stories
- Daily Experiments
- Aspirational Challenges
- Feedback Solicitation
- Milestones Journey
- Plan to Fail
- Celebrate Achievements

Visualize Success

Change resilience is not just a mindset. It requires action and planning. In the last chapter, you began to explore how the change would affect your daily routine. Now it's time to start visualizing success.

By clearly stating your vision, you'll be taking a big step toward turning your intentions into actions. Start by painting a clear picture of success – then move backward to identify the steps to get there.

What do you need to stop doing? What do you need to start doing? What steps are required to achieve this journey? The clearer the operational plan you document and practise, the greater your likelihood of succeeding.

Whenever I work with call centres, I meet people who don't feel their work has much impact. They spend their days dealing with often-disgruntled customers, then they go home. I remind them that the average call-centre employee takes 10,000 calls a year, which might make them understand their impact a bit better, but not much. Then I ask them to envision themselves standing at the centre of a stadium filled with 10,000 people crying out "Help me!" This visual always get them: it reminds them just how powerful they are, the difference they make in so many people's lives.

One of my teams worked with an airline client to develop an interesting program based on the same general principle. Just as frequent fliers rack up airline miles, airline employees collect millions of customers. With every flight, they make more of an impact, and we celebrate when employees reach 100,000 customers, 500,000 customers, 750,000, and then one million served.

But impact need not be solely quantitative. When working with another company, we created a storytelling competition, bringing customers in to talk about the impact the company has had on their lives. Simply by asking customers about the difference you've made in someone's life, you start seeing that you are much more powerful than you think.

Visualize success.

To fully own the transformation, you need to know what success looks like. Consider:

1. Imagine you've fully operationalized new habits and behaviours. What do you look like? Where would you be?

2. What would your customers' response be?

3. How would your customers feel?

4. What would they share with others?

5. Share some details of your success – perhaps a client refers a friend, or your manager gives you an exciting new project.

6. Imagine what you should stop doing.

7. Imagine what you should start doing.

Start This, Stop This

At the most basic level, change is about replacing old habits, behaviours and thought patterns with new ones. One of our clients came up with great wish lists of behaviours they'd need to start – and those they'd need to stop – in order to fully operationalize change. Use their insights to inspire your own list.

START:

+ Focusing on the power we do have

+ Understanding our customers' emotions first

+ Recognizing that the future is already here

+ Understanding that change is a process

+ Asking the right questions

+ Strengthening our cause

+ Being creative

+ Adding value in every interaction

+ Realizing it's okay to be afraid

+ Being proud of our emotions

+ Focusing on our impact

+ Making change intrinsic

STOP:

- ✦ Focusing on transactions

- ✦ Declaring victory before the customer is happy

- ✦ Treating customers as a means to an end

- ✦ Keeping the existing process at all costs

- ✦ Repeating yesterday's performance

- ✦ Sticking to old convictions

- ✦ Ignoring people's emotions

Create Daily Rituals

Have you ever seen a football team hitting the field without a huddle first? No! The huddle is part of the prep work necessary to align hearts and minds and win the game. Spending time in a tight circle aligns the whole team around their mission. Those who bring conviction and passion to the huddle are more likely to feel connected to their fellow players during the game.

Your daily performance is no different. A passionate, authentic daily ritual will get you aligned and connected. That's why my teams refer to our daily rituals as 'huddles'. Here's a basic rundown of what our huddles look like:

The daily huddle.

1. Review your core cause.

2. Review the change that's taking place and how it affects operations.

3. Review yesterday's performance.

4. Note the lessons learned from yesterday's performance.

5. Review the impact the change has had on people's lives.

6. Discuss emotional readiness of each employee to serve people.

7. Plan and commit to today's performance.

Huddles should not take more than 15 minutes. Schedule them first thing in the morning to help you focus your efforts on doing work that's in alignment with your core cause.

Don't forget to review yesterday's performance and keep track of what you learned. Every day's performance plays an integral role in building up your change resilience. Learn from your failures and celebrate your successes. Every step on this journey matters.

Whenever I talk about the importance of daily rituals with a new client, I get the same reaction: "We can't do it every day. Is it possible to skip some days?"

"Sure," I respond. "You may skip the daily huddle every day that you are willing to compromise your performance. On those days, feel free to skip it."

The manager of a sustainability initiative was reluctant to introduce anything like a daily huddle to his team because he'd tried a similar technique in the past and failed.

So I asked him: *Why* had it failed?

As it turned out, his team had simply sent a memo to all front-line supervisors explaining what a daily huddle was and advising them to start using them. Unfortunately, not many people feel comfortable speaking in front of others. Many more do not know what a huddle in a business context looks like. No wonder the practice never took off!

Building this kind of ritual – or introducing any new technique or tool – requires confidence and practise. Without repetition, we get distracted and veer from the plan. Without practise, an intense commitment to the plan will melt into a lukewarm 'going through the motions'.

Daily rituals remind us of our commitment, reinforce the rationale behind it and demonstrate that we are making progress. They should refocus your attention on your core cause and remind you of what you need to do differently to bring your commitment to life.

We also need daily rituals to celebrate progress. Reflect on the impact you're making as a result of the change. Draw strength from the power you have and the inspiration you create.

While some may perceive daily rituals as redundant, we find them critical to success. Organizations that embrace daily huddles or jump-starts experience a higher level of employee engagement and focus around mission and values.

Plan to Fail

Yes, you read that correctly. Just a few pages after asking you to visualize success, I'm challenging you to plan for failure. Why?

Because you will.

Because no journey is a straight line between intention and success.

Because we are human and we have weak moments.

Because there are always unexpected occurrences that will throw us off our game.

And because we need to be ready to get back on track when all this happens.

Most people do not plan to fail – they try to power through to success on sheer commitment and willpower alone. But, as behavioural economist Dan Ariely has written, willpower is a muscle that can get tired over time. When that happens, we tend to cheat on our diets, miss a day at the gym and go back to all those bad habits we thought we'd kicked.

We need to recognize the temptations, time pressures and inevitable obstacles, and accept them. We will fail on our journey. We can also forgive ourselves – as long as we know we are ready to get back on track.

So plan to fail.

Accept it.

And keep going.

Create reinforcement visuals.

What's your screen saver?

✦ Consider changing it to reflect your commitment
to change.

How about the photo on your desk, the magnet on your fridge?

✦ Just as daily rituals are verbal reminders to stick to the
plan, reinforcement visuals emphasize your commitment.
Think creatively: use a new luggage tag for your bag, a
new sticker for your laptop. Make your vision visible.

Capture the Success Stories

As you venture on the road to personal or professional transformation, you're going to achieve a number of quantitative objectives.
But first you will experience qualitative progress. Do not ignore that
progress. In fact, oftentimes I encourage our clients to focus on the
qualitative results even more than the quantitative ones.

A qualitative result is a story about the impact you've created. These reaffirming stories build your character, confidence and commitment to continue on the journey toward transformation.

Before you try to change the whole world, change one person's world.

As we were working on the Mercedes-Benz transformation, we collected thousands of inspiring stories from the field. But one story stuck with me:

The story begins on a Long Island highway. Cue the heavy rain. A car washer who worked at a local Mercedes-Benz dealership saw one of their models on the side of the road. He stopped and asked if the driver needed help.

"I'm good," said the driver. "I'm waiting for roadside assistance."

"Well, in that case, please allow me to just stand by you until they arrive," the car washer said. "I don't want any of our family members to be alone during such a time."

Without getting paid for this gesture, he stayed outside in the rain out of a sense of personal duty to the people whom he works with and for. He made the choice to treat a customer as part of his extended family.

It was simple. It was powerful. It was human. It was a person who was seeking to make an impact right then and there.

Write your own book of stories like this, and they will fuel your passion and commitment and lift you during the down moments. We become future ready by making an impact one life at a time.

Daily Experiments

Remember the study I shared about musical taste stagnating at age 33? The same is true of other aspects of our lives. We settle down on our favourite food, beer, news feed, social tool – and often stop trying much else.

But when we stop experimenting, we stop evolving.

One way to get yourself future ready is to start experimenting in different areas of your life. Let's start with fonts: I bet that, like the majority of people using Times Roman or Arial, you ignore 99% of the fonts available to you. It's time to try some new styles.

And when was the last time you tried a new PowerPoint template? Animation? Or *any* new feature, for that matter?

CHANGE RESILIENCE CHALLENGE #11

Dedicate 15 minutes of your day to experimenting with the tools you already use. Need a reminder? Try new passwords. What about 'TryNewThings' or 'WhatsNext'? Words like this help you kick off your day with an experimental mindset.

Push yourself – but do so gently. As you explore the new change you committed to, don't just stick to the plan. As you see that you start reaching your goals, extend your boundaries bit by bit. Explore new ideas.

I've made it a habit to explore one new website a day. To learn something I didn't know. It can be as simple as listening to a TED Talk about a new subject. Regular visits to crowdfunding sites like Kickstarter and Indiegogo also help me flex my change muscles. Check out what people are inventing. You might think some ideas are stupid. But others may inspire you.

The goal is to keep exploring.

Stay curious.

Solicit Feedback

Feedback is funny. Everyone welcomes it as long as it is positive and makes us feel good. But negative feedback? Despite our attempts to disguise it as 'constructive,' we hate it.

I'm not immune. When a participant in one of our sessions wrote a nasty comment about something I'd said, I was hurt. The fact that the majority of the participants loved the workshop didn't matter. I let that one negative voice cloud my perception of the whole event. (I am not proud of this, but I know it was a human reaction.) It took me some time to reflect and understand where that participant was coming from.

Ask people for honest feedback. Invite them to rate – and even coach. Except for those who suffer from an acute inferiority complex, most of us rate our own performance as above average and declare victory before it is achieved. Let others help you reflect more accurately and support your progress.

You can use formal surveys or simply ask the people you work with how you are progressing:

+ Do they notice something new?

+ Were they expecting something different?

+ Does your behaviour seem authentic or fake?

Let the people you are trying to impact guide you on the journey. A final few words of advice about feedback:

+ Listen carefully to everything they've said.

+ Don't just gravitate to the negative feedback.
  Ask people to let you know what you do well,
  not just criticize what you are missing.

Positive and negative feedback come hand in hand. And you will need the positive to support your efforts to improve what you still need to work on. Positive feedback will build your confidence and enable you to face the areas that need improvement with the right attitude. So listen to everything, and accept it all.

Celebrate Success – Reward Yourself

For success to last, it needs to be visible. Just as it is important to assign goals and a time frame for our targets, it is equally critical to celebrate when we reach those milestones. Reward yourself for sticking to the change plan and making it this far. At every milestone, take some action to make success visible and celebrate it.

What makes a good reward? It depends on you. It does not have to be expensive, but make sure it is memorable and supports your goals in some way.

One European logistics company could not reward employees with anything of monetary value because of union regulations – so they got creative. The company's number-one asset was its fleet of thousands of trucks. Employees who exceeded customers' expectations got to have a truck named after them for a month. They felt like a million dollars (okay, maybe euros), yet it did not cost anything to implement the program. It was inspirational, memorable and aspirational. Other employees upped their game because they wanted the same recognition.

The cynic in you may say, "I'd rather have more money," but the truth is that money does not have the same impact. Extra cash will be spent quickly on basic necessities and forgotten very quickly. Memorable experiences carry a far greater impact and make for a more sharable story.

Be creative with your rewards – and make sure that achievement does not go unnoticed. Celebrating success is about reinforcing the plan and ensuring its future success.

Live the transformation.

A t this point, you've been testing your new behaviour in small
ways and begun experimenting in your daily life. Now it's time to
start living the transformation. But just as if you were training for a
marathon, you need to create a plan.

In the last chapter, you began to understand how change would
affect the larger ecosystem that you're part of — your customers and
the people you interact with on a regular basis. The next step is to
build on that by noting how you can hold yourself accountable and
reward yourself. Part of that is setting up a system of support — who
are the people and the resources you will use to keep you on track?
Whom will you turn to when the going gets tough?

	What would you do?	How often?	Who would support you?
Visualize Success			
Visual Reminders			
Daily Rituals			
Success Stories			
Daily Experimentations			
Aspirational Challenges			
Milestones Journey			
Feedback Solicitation			
Plan to Fail			
Celebrate Achievements			

After setting up the plan, review your progress regularly,
adapt your plan when necessary — and don't forget to celebrate
your success!

The Power to Reinvent

Change resilience is not a destination, but a lifestyle. Change rushes at us constantly, and if we don't want to drown, we need to go with the flow.

What distinguishes people from animals is our ability to imagine and create. We have the resources to come up with new ideas and bring them into being. We have the power to reinvent the world. A world with advanced medicine is a better world. A world with breakthrough transportation is a world reaching farther. A world with art is a more beautiful world.

Humans are creators. Humans change the world. And the transformation should never stop. Yes, some have changed the world for the worse. I would argue that what unites many of history's most infamous tyrants is that they lacked the core cause of making a positive difference in the world – not just for themselves but for others.

The world will never stop changing. So we must continue to ask ourselves: What is the next big change? How does it impact my core cause? What should I start doing? What should I stop?

We have the opportunity to approach every transformation from a position of strength. It requires asking: How will it better enable me to achieve my core cause? To answer that question, it helps to understand what will stay the same and what will not. Every time a new challenge or scenario presents itself, ask yourself two questions:

✦ What will stay the same?

Answers might include your values, your achievements to date, the people you serve. The point of asking this question is to remember the strengths you've already established.

✦ What will shift?

The shift you're about to experience may be small – for instance, establishing a new social communication channel. Or it may be as significant as rethinking your whole model for engaging with new potential clients and customers. Either way, your established strengths and skills will help you transition into the new way of doing things.

Ask these questions with your core cause in mind. Doing so will strengthen your change resilience, ensuring that while the tools of your job might change, your mission and values will not.

PART THREE

ten

LEADING CHANGE RESILIENCE

In just 90 days, two pharmaceutical companies would merge two divisions to create a leader in their space. In preparation, 18 people from different parts of the world met to discuss a new employee web portal. A representative from each department spoke up:

+ The IT team raised concerns about the portal hosting.

+ The security team shared a 90-page document on compliance.

+ The marketing team demanded that the portal reflect the new brand.

✦ HR shared their concern about employees'
readiness for this big change.

As I observed the conversation, it hit me. Each department stuck to a script of what could go wrong. No one was empowered to make decisions. In other words, all the naysayers were present, but not a single person with the power to say yes was in attendance.

No one seemed to care about the big picture at all. Each participant was interested only in protecting his or her own turf by raising red flags. The fact that a multibillion-dollar merger was on the line didn't seem to faze them. They were passively rejecting change and hiding behind their processes and procedures. If only the new CEO had been there to see how ill-equipped for change his team was!

While mergers and acquisitions present an extreme case of disruption, they share many characteristics with other change efforts, and therefore illustrate the urgent need for change-resilient leadership. When people adopt this kind of tunnel vision, every strategy and change is at risk of failing or losing momentum.

In this chapter, we're going to focus on how to lead change. It's filled with advice from some leaders who don't just passively accept change, but who live and breathe it. It's a crucial chapter for leaders of teams and organizations, but also for everyone committed to change. After all, you must take a proactive role in changing your own behaviour. That will mean sitting in the CEO's seat and holding yourself accountable to your vision.

There's another reason to put yourself in the leader's role. If you start making positive changes in your life, you can bet people will start asking how you did it. Here's your opportunity to think about how to scale your efforts so that you can help others live their core causes.

This requires you to think about how the change will affect those around you and how to bring others on board to support your efforts. How are you building trust and leading people to change? Are they mentally, intellectually and operationally ready to leave behind old practices and deliver the Next?

Are you?

Know Your Ecosystem

In the world of performing arts, Deborah Rutter is regarded as a true change agent. As I write, she is on her third mission – this time, leading a new initiative at the John F. Kennedy Center for the Performing Arts in Washington, DC. As the CEO of the centre, she is working to leverage its rich heritage while ensuring its continued relevance.

In the past, guests of the centre defined culture as ballet or classical music performances, whereas today the definition has expanded to include street art and participatory theatrical experiences.

Rutter arrived at the Kennedy Center after completing successful transformations with the Seattle Symphony and the Chicago Symphony Orchestra. Her first piece of advice?

"Know your cultural ecosystem." In other words, change resilience ought to be developed based on what is natural to people and, therefore, intrinsic. Do not attempt to change who anyone is; rather, make sure your initiatives take into consideration their beliefs and values – and build from there.

"Seattle is a very different city from Chicago," Rutter explains. "Understanding the cultural foundation will enable a leader to act differently and amplify the change based on who they naturally are."

While Seattle is all about independence, what makes Chicago tick is its bootstrap nature. The cities naturally require different approaches to transformation. Rutter also recognizes that the Kennedy Center serves several distinct groups – the local, national and international communities. Each has its own characteristics and requires that the change feel natural to them.

Rutter and other veterans of successful change initiatives advise: be realistic. Do not just read change success stories and assume you can copy another company's every move. While I enjoyed reading about Tony Hsieh's success with Zappos in *Delivering Happiness: A Path to Profits, Passion, and Purpose*, I knew that it bore little relevance to most companies. Why?

Because the DNA of Zappos is not the DNA of every other company. Some organizations would reject Hsieh's advice as if it were toxic. The reason it worked for Zappos was that Hsieh assembled people whose personalities fit that specific culture. He also opted to take $36,000 a year as a CEO salary. The average CEO must go through something like $36,000 in expenses per week!

The change resilience of any organization ought to be an integral and natural extension of the organization's identity. Start with the culture you have and build on that.

As for individuals, take into account your own habits and culture. If your family used to bond over big Sunday dinners, for example, you might bring your love of breaking bread with family into your routine. You don't need to eliminate what you love – just replace some of the dishes with healthier options.

Change resilience isn't about throwing out what we love – it's about building on it.

The Sum Total of Everyone's Decisions

In a world of diminishing centralized authority and growing distributed authorities, leaders often ignore a simple truth that is right in front of them. Their organization is the sum total of their employees' decisions. It is Susan from Accounting and David from Operations and Jane from Sales and Sean from Customer Service who every day make hundreds of decisions that shape the future of the organization. They are the new authorities in a world distrustful of authority. Leaders need to accept the fact that their role is not to decide, but rather to empower decisions. After all, it is not the BIG decision made in the boardroom that matters much. It is the millions of small decisions employees make every day that activate the desired change in many ways.

When employees are inspired and empowered, change will be accelerated. If employees are cynical and restricted, change will drag out until it becomes irrelevant.

Leadership is about activating the causes of employees and aligning them with a vision, tools and the confidence to drive the transformation. It is about leveraging the newly discovered authority within each employee to the point of collectively making a difference.

Success Isn't Guaranteed

Eric became CEO of a national distribution company the old-fashioned way. After decades of devoted service to the company, he'd risen through the ranks. He was known to be a shrewd operator and he was no stranger to change – he'd already lived through several different incarnations of the company. He was also deeply analytical – the kind of guy who'd make red marks on every slide. So when we presented our strategy for growth to him, he'd already run his own analysis.

"I'll sign off on this strategy if you can guarantee me a success," he told us.

"Anyone who will guarantee you a success in transformation is either selling a commonsense idea they already shared with your competitors," I said, "or they are lying."

I am surprised at how frequently even the most accomplished people forget what change is all about. Transformation is, by definition, risky. You are attempting to do something you've never done.

You don't know how it will work. That is part of the excitement and the fear.

When you repeat something you've always done, on the other hand, that's safe. Unfortunately, it's also no longer special or distinctive. You can't have it both ways. If you want the excitement of the new, you must assume the fear of the unknown.

Here's how a couple of change veterans do that:

I. Don't start with a complete plan.

Steve Cannon is the former CEO of Mercedes-Benz USA and the current CEO of AMB Group – the company that owns the Atlanta Falcons. His words of wisdom about change?

"You can't have a complete plan when you start."

Yes, you need a clear vision of the future – but be prepared to build on it as you go. You need to learn from your mistakes, try new things and experiment. That is the only way to transform. No consulting firm can provide you with the complete strategy in advance.

Cannon is currently working on redefining the fan experience at the new Atlanta Falcons stadium. His greatest competitor?

"You can enjoy the game on an 80-inch TV at home," he told me. "Why bother coming to the stadium?"

What does the new live sports look like? How can it be miles beyond the televised version (especially when you take into account Atlanta's notorious traffic jams)? While I'm sure Cannon will come up with something exciting and unexpected, you can bet it will combine elements that will need to be tested and refined.

Rutter echoed Cannon's belief that you can't map out your entire change journey on day one.

"How could you possibly know the future?" she asked. "To assume a fixed, predefined strategy is simply not realistic."

Just as you expect your people to be patient and open-minded about change, be honest with yourself. Transformation is an open road: you know where you want to get to, but have few clues about how to get there. Let your culture guide you.

2. Fix the trust gap.

The gap between what leadership promises to do and what they *actually* do is probably one of the most significant challenges to executing a successful transformation. Over time, that gap will devolve into eroded trust.

"We are planning to instill a Nordstrom culture here," a CEO told me. He was referring to *The Nordstrom Way*, the book about how the retailer gained its reputation for excellent customer service. "I have read the book and I am ready to do it. It will not be optional. Everyone will have to buy into it," he continued enthusiastically as we walked through one of his bigger stores.

I reached into my pants pocket, pulled out a tissue and, much to his surprise, threw it on the floor.

"What are you doing?" he asked me.

"Pick it up, please," I said.

"Let me arrange for someone to clean it up."

"The CEO of Nordstrom would have no problem picking a piece of trash up off the floor," I said. "He wouldn't need to arrange for someone to do it for him."

This story speaks to the heart of the challenge that leadership faces during transformation. It is not that leaders fail to declare change. They do that abundantly well and with boisterous words. It's that they fail to convince people and, even worse, fail to become the role models for change. Give them the text and they will recite it to the last word. Ask them to take action and you will see them squirm.

I once worked with a Japanese executive who considered himself enlightened. He told me that loving the customer was essential in his company. He even paid for his executives to partake in a program at the Disney Institute. But when I suggested that he call one customer a day to thank them for their business – a practice that would take less than five minutes – his attitude completely changed. He was unhappy with the recommendation and considered it unreasonable for someone so busy.

Change often fails because employees simply do not trust leadership's commitment to transform. They see leaders asking them to change but refusing to change themselves. Employees follow actions, not words.

If you're serious about developing change resilience among your employees, you must build their trust and convince them that the new change is for real and is here to stay. Plenty of programs-du-jour come and go. Employees live to see them evaporate after a magnificent – and often expensive – launch. The launch-and-abandon graveyard is full of great intentions that never materialized. No wonder so many employees take a wait-and-see approach to change. They expect their leaders to take the lead.

CHANGE RESILIENCE CHALLENGE #12

People won't follow you if they don't trust you. If you're leading a transformation, ask: "How can I demonstrate that I am personally committed to change?"

What actions will you take to convince the cynics that 'this time is different'? What will you do to shock them into belief? The credibility factor is critical. Only when your people believe you will they follow you.

3. Don't let change blockers derail you.

If you've gotten this far in a transformation, you've likely identified some change blockers. While you try to steer the ship to the left, they are desperately holding you back by steering it to the right. They do not agree with your vision. They are not interested in change. They have a different vision of the future – a return to the good old days.

Maybe you've already gotten them on board. But if you're anything like most of the people my teams work with, you are avoiding them. If that's the case, you can and should try to make them understand and believe in your position. But eventually you will realize there's no room in the organization for the change-resistant – and that epiphany will come sooner than you think.

First you'll try to change your actions and become a role model, but that will win over only a portion of the change blockers.

That will be your moment of truth – the moment when you need to say good-bye to those who refuse to join the movement you are trying to create.

It is not going to be easy. Nostalgia will take hold and try to convince you to keep them. Don't let it. They are not here to change with the times. They are here to keep the status quo – and in so doing, they will jeopardize the entire company. They have no right to do it. The only reason they've gotten this far is because you let them.

Whether you're a leader grappling with cynical voices in your organization or an individual struggling with unsupportive people in your life or naysayers in your head, the responsibility to remove them is on you. Keep in mind that everyone else is watching. The resisters are working behind your back in staff meetings and lunches and informal conversations you are not part of. Or they are making decisions to thwart your efforts. They procrastinate and delay to no end the necessary change. If you do not take action – and fast – they will contaminate the motivation and excitement of the rest. You simply cannot afford employees who are dead set against your strategy for the future.

There is no one who can have more of an impact on this situation than you. You become a role model when you remove a change blocker from your ecosystem. You build trust with the rest of the organization. It's not fun, but it is the only way to build a change-resilient personality or organization.

4. Be authentic.

Think back to the last time you tried to get people on board with a new idea.

Maybe you led with some stats or a well-crafted PowerPoint presentation full of charts, arrows and numbers. Then, after a series of questions that you managed to dodge, right before you were about to present your closing remarks and declare the meeting a victory, you slid in something about social impact.

Now, let's be honest. What message did you send when 90% of your talk focused on your pride in the latest figures, and less than one minute was dedicated to a rushed message about the impact the company had on human beings? Is that really a commitment to a cause or just lip service?

People are very astute when it comes to noticing what's important to others. We pay attention not to words but to actions, passion, pride. Are you invested in your cause or in your numbers? What really matters to you? Where is your heart?

Too many leaders see themselves as Guardians of the Process. They mostly communicate the numbers, trends, statistics, percentages and financial goals. Listen even more carefully and you will note what you do not hear: their core cause.

Here is a reality check: people don't change for the numbers. You want people to feel ready to change? Start talking about the cause. As a leader, you must be the bearer of the cause torch. The numbers can help bolster your argument, but they should not be the endgame.

Every meeting, every town hall, every conversation is an opportunity to talk about your commitment to your cause. You should repeat it as many times as possible. People need to believe you are truly committed for the long haul. Remember, people will be skeptical about your seriousness. Thanks to years of number-crunching, they expect change initiatives to be short-lived. You must win them over, and it will not be easy.

Whatever you do, be authentic. Tell personal stories, not someone else's story. If you find yourself thinking, *This will be great PR*, take a step back. Let other people make the call about whether your initiative is newsworthy or not. It's your job to be genuine.

5. Own the conversation.

Remember AMB CEO Steve Cannon? He has another valuable piece of advice about leading change:

"Your most important role is to own the conversation. If change resilience is what you are seeking, make sure everyone knows it. Weave it into every presentation and communication. Increase the frequency of the conversation and make sure everyone is speaking the same message."

The biggest mistake leaders make is to assume that if they say something once, people will immediately do it. Nothing could be further from the truth. When you say something once, people will doubt it – if they hear you at all. When you say it twice, they may listen a little longer – and still dismiss it. When you repeat it for the third time, they will start paying attention. By about the tenth time you say it, they may actually consider doing something about it.

Before you have a complete operational plan in effect, you should have a clear and comprehensive communication plan. Your employees, colleagues, friends and family hear new ideas every day. You'd be surprised how few of them understand your strategy or where you want to go – and I'm not even talking about the change-resistant who are actively trying to thwart your ideas. (You haven't let them go yet? What are they still doing here?)

Develop a communication plan and make it clear there is no time for hesitation. Use every possible 'real estate' space available – both physical and virtual – to communicate your message. And when you advocate for change, do not forget to express what *doesn't* change.

Make it easy for others to tell their stories about how they're embracing change. You can do this whether you're a leader at an established organization, an activist hoping to launch a new social movement or a marketing consultant seeking more subscribers to your newsletter. Here are a few simple strategies:

+ Create videos featuring top executives, influential members of your community or people with powerful stories sharing their vision of transformation.

+ Share your message at a panel or workshop.

+ Set up a meeting or event to share your message.

Whatever your format is – and the more, the merrier – make sure your message is unified. Doing so will remove any doubts as to where you're headed. It will help those on the fence – the helpless, the curious and the hopeless – to make up their minds and, most importantly, take action.

Every transformation is different. As much as you may want to schedule and plan every step of it ahead of time, you need to be ready for the unknown. In this kind of organic, authentic, 'no script' transformation, conversation is your most effective tool to align and rally people toward the future. The more transparency and commitment displayed by you and your team, the greater the chance of getting others on board.

Be honest and sincere and do not make promises you cannot keep. Make sure everyone understands that the transformation is a journey. Don't fake confidence – people will pick up on it and you'll lose them. However, you should show how passionate you feel about the future. Explain the *why*. Invite others to experiment and share their progress. Make it clear this is a conversation.

6. Be relentless about pursuing What's Next.

"In our company, we are all empowered to make the *right* decision."

This was one employee's response to a question about empowerment. The other employees in the focus group giggled. They knew exactly what that person meant. In an organization where employees are only empowered to make the *right* decision, everyone defaults to the safest option – the one we used yesterday. The only way to avoid making mistakes is to avoid making decisions.

Take an honest look at yourself/your organization: Do you reward yourself and your employees for repetition or for exploration? For trying something different or for being compliant? If you've built a strong culture of trust, you can very easily introduce new transformation initiatives without a detailed strategy. Instead of commanding others, you empower them to jump on board when you introduce new ideas. You also empower them to deliver amazing service that goes above and beyond.

I was standing outside the Four Seasons Hotel in Los Angeles when the doorman engaged me in a simple conversation.

"How are you enjoying your stay with us so far?" he asked.

"There were some good things and some bad things," I replied.

"What were the bad things?" he immediately asked. "I want a chance to fix the bad things first."

He wrote down my points of contention and referred them directly to the right person. Later that day I had a letter of apology and an assortment of fruit waiting for me in my room. Needless to say, I was impressed.

I would expect that type of response from the general manager, not the doorman. The issues I'd experienced were not in his area of responsibility; nevertheless, he felt a sense of ownership. He listened and acted immediately. What impressed me most was the fact that he downplayed the good things I'd experienced. For him, the good things were a given. It was what they could do better that mattered the most to him.

Performing this way requires a sense of pride and ownership and a focus on improvement. The doorman wasn't afraid of taking a complaint because change and improvement were natural to him. This kind of 'we can always do better' attitude is the cornerstone of a change resilience culture.

I think of change resilience as "a relentless pursuit of What's Next."

When a relentless pursuit of the Next becomes an integral part of employees' daily activities, you are creating a change-resilient culture. That way, when big changes come, your team will be ready. Culture is the result of the daily choices of every employee. It is a group of people who share a vision and passion, who act despite uncertainty and create exceptional experiences one action at a time. You don't need a one-size-fits-all process when you share a vision.

A change-resilient culture never accepts the status quo or yesterday's success. It's a culture of curiosity: seeking new ideas through customers' comments, employees' ideas, new technology and competitors' moves.

7. Quit seeking out a perfect 10.

Want a simple litmus test for how change resilient your culture is? Look at your customer satisfaction programs. Many customer satisfaction surveys look more like a scorecard seeking a perfect 10. Companies look for validation that their performance was, in fact, good.

It's almost desperate.

Imagine if, instead, in the next survey you asked questions to find out what else you could have done to make the experience or performance better: What were the missed opportunities? What else could we have done to delight you?

Such a survey would give you much richer insights about how to 'Create the Next'.

It might not be the perfect score you were seeking, but it could be instead the key to your future.

QUICK GUIDE

QUICK GUIDE: TEN PRINCIPLES FOR CREATING A CHANGE-RESILIENT CULTURE

1. **Focus on the core cause.** If all employees are connected to your mission, they will deliver the desired outcome their way – and in the best way possible. Keep them connected to the cause and let them lead the way.

2. **Demonstrate your personal commitment to change.** How will you build trust among your employees and demonstrate your commitment to the proposed change? What will you do differently?

3. **Start every interaction by asking "What's next?"** Establish a curiosity in everything you do. Always ask for a better way. Experiment with new tools. Start the conversation with the question "What's next?"

4. **Highlight what doesn't change.** Your mission and values usually do not change. Give employees the comfort of knowing that even amid change, some things stay constant. The values and mission that brought them to your organization will continue to guide the future and serve as a bridge between the past and the new vision you're advocating.

5. **Set expectations.** This is a journey with unpredictable turns. While we know the endgame, the milestones and efforts to get there are merely an estimation. There will be pleasant and some less-than-pleasant surprises on the journey. Employees should get ready for a ride and should not expect to have all the answers beforehand.

6. **Seek improvement – not validation.** Ditch the validating surveys and focus on improvement. Ask different stakeholders to guide you to unmet needs, missed opportunities and aspirational yet unfulfilled dreams – anything that can highlight the next opportunity.

7. **Emphasize ownership of the outcome.** By freeing people to do things their way but holding them accountable to timelines and outcome, you increase their responsibility. They now own the process and need to find the best way to get to the outcome. When you control

QUICK GUIDE

the entire process, they lack any ownership since they are doing it your way, not theirs.

8. **Recognize the differences between employees' styles.** Publicly recognize the different execution styles of different employees. Validate their approaches and recognize that there is more than one way to obtain the outcome. Inspire employees to share practices and exchange ideas.

9. **Encourage experimentation.** Conduct sessions that focus on tweaking the way you do business. Just because it works doesn't mean there isn't a better way. Formalize the pursuit of the Next through monthly or quarterly mini-innovation sessions.

10. **Celebrate innovation.** Institutionalize your innovators. Establish a recognition program for those who have tried but have yet to succeed. Celebrate those who have introduced new technologies or found new improvements. Make constant improvement an integral part of the organization's heritage. A company innovation museum, anyone?

Nurturing Employee Engagement

Now that we've covered some strategies for building a culture of change resilience, let's look at some ways you can continue to support and empower your teams.

How powerful do those on your team feel? As if they can conquer the world or are like cogs in the machine? As a leader, your main purpose is to help others reach new heights of performance. The more they achieve, the better your results will be. Consider the following techniques to create a culture of engagement:

1. Set aspirational goals to motivate them.
   What is the next 'exceptional' for them?

2. Identify the tools they need to succeed and
   empower them to accomplish their goals.

3. Provide a safety net that allows them to feel
   comfortable to experiment and do things
   they've never done before.

Leading with your core cause will provide the *why*. The next step is to set employees up to succeed in accomplishing their objectives.

The question "How can I help you reach higher?" cannot wait for an annual performance review. Smart companies are abandoning this practice and encouraging leaders to engage in frequent conversations about that question. But the questioning process is only part of it – you also need to set aspirational goals that challenge employees to step out of their comfort zone.

Instead of creating and enforcing a one-size-fits-all process, give people breathing room to make the change their own. Recognize that everyone may reach the goals you set differently, but as long as they seek to fulfil the same cause, different executions are welcome. The cause is the unifier, but the tools may vary. Ownership should take precedence over process.

Sharing Impact with Those Working Behind the Scenes

During a customer-experience training with employees from a pharmaceutical company, one participant raised his hand and asked to be excused. He was part of the IT team and saw no need to sit through training on customer experience.

"What are you working on?" I asked him.

"I am part of the SAP implementation team," he replied. "It has nothing to do with customers. It's a back-end system."

"Why is the company allocating millions of dollars to implement an SAP system?" I asked.

"I don't know" was his answer.

"Who is your internal buyer?" I asked. "Would you please check for me why they are investing in the SAP system?"

After a few phone calls, he returned with the following story: "The company is investing in SAP in order to better understand their costs. They hope to be able to develop a better pricing model so they can penetrate business in countries where their drugs are currently too expensive."

"How many patients are affected or can use your drugs in those countries?" I asked.

"Fifty million" was his reply.

And at that moment, he got it. His work affected 50 million suffering patients. Just because he didn't see or speak to patients directly didn't mean he was not part of the cause. SAP was his tool. But his cause was to help patients who could not get access to the drugs they needed due to high costs.

I don't blame him for initially wanting out of the session. In team meetings, his leaders measured progress using timeline and budget metrics. They buried themselves in spreadsheets, graphs and charts. They never contextualized the project or spoke about the impact that the project would have on people's lives – which is kind of odd for a pharmaceutical company dedicated to saving lives.

Fifty million patients is an impact. Yet no one focused on that. Because talk centred on tactical goals, no one saw the face of the patient in need. No one was connected to the company's core cause.

It doesn't matter what kind of initiative you're leading – your core cause ought to be the central theme in every conversation you have with your team. Every bit of conversation should start and end with the human impact. If your organization does not serve customers directly or only provides back-office support, then sharing impact becomes even more critical. Consider the following strategies:

+ Use stories or customer testimonials to make the impact on customers clear to everyone at your organization.

+ Every completed task should include a description of the impact it made on real people who live with the outcome of the team's work.

+ Weave a human story into every presentation of financial or operational results.

Let's face it – a lot of leaders are trained to measure success using charts and graphs. But that's not what moves people to change. You need to make sure everyone from the front line to the assembly line understands how his or her actions affect customers.

Do the Human Thing First

"No matter what happens, do the human thing first." This is the mantra that all of my employees live by. They know I have their backs when they do the human thing. There is no way you can go wrong by sending a bouquet of flowers with your condolences to a client who recently experienced a death in the family. You will never be criticized for making a donation to your client's favourite charity after making a mistake. No need to ask for permission. Just do it and hand us the expense report. We will pay for it.

When you live by your core cause, doing the human thing first becomes almost as natural as breathing. Put people first and the rest will follow. Employees who know that their organization puts people first will be more apt to act responsibly and proactively – even in the most challenging moments.

In December 2009, I faced my toughest business challenge. It was my company's worst year – and we weren't alone. Millions of businesses were struggling through the great recession and none of us had a textbook for how to deal with it.

On 1 January 2009, I'd realized we had enough orders to stay in business if I tightened the budget belt. By 30 January, 90% of those orders had been canceled. Not because our services were no longer needed, but simply because companies panicked and backed out, assuming we wouldn't go after them for breach of contract since everyone was in deep financial trouble. I had no idea what to do.

My anxiety was high and I was all out of ideas. Many sleepless nights didn't provide an answer, only more fears and desperation. I had a family to take care of. My oldest daughter was going to college. How would I pay for that? I had employees and their families who depended on me for their livelihood. The burden of leading others was never as heavy as it was that year. It felt like everything might collapse in a matter of seconds.

During 2009, several employees approached me and said they knew that if I fired them, the chances of the company's survival would increase. They saw me laboring to stay afloat. I ended up reducing employees' salaries in order to keep the team together. Budgets were cut drastically, and I doubled our efforts to find new business.

We survived while some of our competitors reduced in size or scope or disappeared altogether. We even made a modest profit as the year drew to a close. But the visibility for 2010 was still cloudy and unclear. Everything was shaky.

Then, that December, the moment of truth occurred.

We have a company tradition that began the year I started the company. At the end of every year, each employee receives money from the company to donate to his or her charity of choice. At our holiday party each year, every employee proudly discusses the charity they chose – it's a way for us all to connect with each other's core causes.

Now, I would rather have kept the year's profits to finance 2010. Every dollar mattered – a lesson I'd learned the hard way in 2009. I had to ask myself: Do I keep the charity tradition alive or not? I reasoned that I could just make a small donation to one charity on behalf of all of us to keep the spirit of the tradition alive – but it didn't feel right. Perhaps I could increase some of the salaries I had initially cut.

Instead, I opted to keep the original tradition of individual donations intact. My message to my team was: "There are people who suffered more than us this year. Let's do the human thing first." I believe it is not our words but rather our actions that speak the loudest – and this was a moment when my values were put to the test.

Do your values supersede everything else, or will you compromise them at the first sight of a challenge? It was both a difficult and an easy decision. The financial issue was ever-present, but the experience of being able to look in the mirror and know that I lived by my values, even in a time of hardship, was priceless.

More than anything else, it became a proof point to all employees who later joined our team: Doing the human thing first is not a slogan. It is who we are. Living by our cause is not a convenience. It is what we do.

Leading a culture of change resilience is about constantly living by your cause. It is living the change you want to see in everyone else. Your actions give others permission to reach for What's Next. It reminds people that adaptation is not about giving up on anything important, but about working with whatever tools you have to live your cause.

Proud to Be Here

In this 140-character-limit era, CEOs often ask for the shortest version of what it means to lead with cause. "How do I know that we're making it?" My answer can be consolidated into a single word: *pride*.

Take a look around you. Are your people proud to be here? And I do not mean just when you participate in a Habitat for Humanity project or during the alcohol-infused holiday party. I am talking about on a day-to-day basis in your office. Do they look happy? Are they sharing their work with pride? Do they see the connection their work has and the impact they are making? Are they smiling? Pride is not a superficial expression we wear in order to stay employed.

Tough times give organizations an opportunity to come together. We all love a crisis. It has this galvanizing power that makes people go above and beyond and show what they are capable of. We rise up to the superhero within us. Give us a superstorm, a terrorist attack or another threat to humankind, and we will be there: creative, passionate and ready to own the cause. No process or procedure can stop us. We will find a work-around for any obstacle.

But where is this passion most of the time? Just sit outside your HQ building and take a look at people's faces at 5pm Do their expressions impart the pride and excitement you saw on their faces that last time the going got rough? Why not? They worked hard today. They showed up for their colleagues and customers. They made an impact.

So what do you think they say as soon as they get home? Do they brag about the impact they made, or do they complain about the bureaucracy?

Pride can help us stay relevant, but when our pride in the past is greater than our pride in our cause, it can hold us back. As a leader, your challenge is to create a sense of pride that will propel people forward. Inspire them to seek new ways to fulfil their promise to their customers. That pride must start with you. I am not talking about producing self-congratulatory videos with tear-jerking images. (I like a powerful story, but stories are not enough.) I am talking about the active pride that creates a sense of urgency to change and improve. I am talking about the pride that destroys obstacles. The pride that makes us challenge our processes every day so we don't get stuck.

Pride is not a passive state of nirvana. It's active and it's powerful. It means empowering everyone to ask: "What's Next?"

Trust Your Conviction

It can be scary leading your organization toward a new vision when you know the path to success will be paved with obstacles. There will be moments of doubt when you wonder if the naysayers' arguments are true. Everyone who's tried to change has encountered them. They're normal, and you are not alone.

As a veteran automobile industry executive, Brian Fulton, the CEO of Mercedes-Benz Canada, is no stranger to change. His biggest piece of advice?

Relax.

"Be confident in your beliefs," says Fulton. "If you are doing it for the right reasons, it will work out. People will recognize the authentic nature of your endeavour and support you.

"Don't try to pull it off too fast and by yourself," he adds, noting the importance of a team that shares your commitment to your cause.

+ Build your inner circle and make sure they are all on board with your vision.

+ Accept that not all of the details are going to be ironed out before you start.

✦ Take the time to develop the internal buy-in
you'll need. It will pay off in the long run.

While doubt will try to take hold in your mind, trust your convictions. Don't be arrogant, but do not lose your confidence either. If your cause is the right cause, and if you are trying to make a difference in people's lives, your team will recognize it. They will see through the fear and recognize that you are trying to do the right thing. Do not let the naysayers beat you down. You will need to hold tight to your belief in your core cause if you want to capture the imagination and commitment of the rest of the team.

Fear and doubts are a natural part of any transformation. Hold on to the cause and stay confident. As doubts try to creep in, recognize that the unknown aspect of transformation can be a source of excitement.

"If I had the recipe already, life would be boring," Fulton concludes. "I enjoy the adventure and the sense of discovery of the unknown."

The Time Is Now

As I was concluding my conversation with Deborah Rutter at the Kennedy Center for the Performing Arts, she said to me, "Here is my last piece of advice: when it comes to change, it is terrible, but if you don't do it, it is worse."

There is never a perfect time for change. We often delay changing in the name of getting the timing, the strategy, the people, the finances, the environment perfectly right. You and I both know there is no such thing as perfect.

Opportunity does not always bang on your door. It gives a quiet little rap. Wait too long to get off the couch and it's gone. If your organization waits for the perfect strategy or timing, you're basically handing the future over to your competitors.

Transformation requires the confidence to operate with incomplete information and deduce from trends what the future will bring. If you wait for complete validation, it will simply be too late.

How fast will you act when change appears on the horizon?

Are you comfortable stepping out in the first ray of light, or do you need the midday sun to convince you of an opportunity?

eleven

LIVING CHANGE RESILIENCE

What do a natural disaster, your best friend's wedding, the death of someone who's close to you and the birth of a child have in common?

They're all situations that inspire us to go out of our way to help others. When significant events both wonderful and terrible occur, people have a way of coming together – of adapting quickly to make an impact.

Every year, as the holiday season approaches, the spirit of charity seems to rise and we feel more generous and obligated to help those less fortunate. Giving comes in many different forms and can range from writing a check to volunteering in a soup kitchen all the way to competing in an extreme sport in support of a cause.

According to the Giving USA Annual Report, in 2015 the average American household gave $2,124 and 71% of all donations were made by individuals. Additionally, 24.9% of Americans have taken part in a volunteering activity.

But we don't just like to give – we also want to see the impact of our gifts, even though this bias means our volunteering efforts are not as powerful as they could be. A 2016 *Wall Street Journal* article titled "The Mistakes We Make When Giving to Charity" points out that people feel that writing a check to a charity is not as meaningful as volunteering in person. According to the authors, the opposite is true; in fact, donating money to a charity often results in a greater impact.

I think this bias presents an untapped opportunity to start making an impact on a larger scale than ever before. What I'm suggesting is a new form of volunteering. While helping the needy in remote locations around the globe is quite important, there are others closer to us who can also benefit from our spirit of charity and generosity – namely, our customers and colleagues. Why is it that people we hardly know command greater attention from us than those who pay us for our services?

In Chapter Four, I revealed one of the most surprising findings from Strativity's survey on engagement: nothing made employees feel more engaged than giving them the chance to deliver a great experience to customers.

People want to feel they can make a difference. So let's tap into this universal spirit of generosity and apply it to our everyday activities. Think about the people on the receiving end of all our actions and make a commitment to making their lives better. Why wait for the annual marathon or the holiday season to make a difference? We can elevate our performance today and every day.

Just imagine how many customers and colleagues your work impacts every year. They need you. They need your absolute best. They are counting on you to understand them, solve their problems, and make their lives easier and better. Even if you do not see customers every day, your work has an effect on them.

It is easy to discover your generous spirit when some life-changing event hits. But do we really need some epic disaster to awaken our compassion? I sure hope not. Remember that everyone you come in contact with has some need. How can you unleash the power of your generosity to help them?

Have you ever wondered why we choose not to be generous with the people we work with? After all, they pay our bills. Based on experience with customer-centric transformations, we've discovered that many employees think they already are acting generously. Others assume that because there's an exchange of money, their work is not truly altruistic. Because they view work as a commercial exchange, they withhold their best efforts. Still others suffer from 'worst customer syndrome'. They judge all customers based on the few outliers who have hurt them in the past –and aren't so quick to be generous.

CHANGE RESILIENCE CHALLENGE #13

It's time to leave the excuses behind. The worst customers should not put us in constant defense mode. It is time to reestablish trust with our customers and treat them all with generosity.

If we start measuring the impact we have on people every day and bring our spirit of generosity to every interaction, we will be pleasantly surprised by the end of the year. The person we see when we look in the mirror will be a better, happier person – and, most of all, a person more proud of who they are and what they do.

Long-Term Change Resilience Strategies

Change resilience is not Usain Bolt's 9.58-second 100-metre dash. It's a lifelong marathon. Running a sprint requires you to focus on the finish as soon as you start running. In a marathon, the finish is less important than your endurance throughout the whole journey.

Remember, change is no longer an event. It is now an integral part of our lives. Treating it as temporary weakens our change resilience and our ability to stay relevant in the world. Living change resilience means constantly training and adapting. In this chapter, I will share strategies for strengthening your change resilience muscles.

1. Never stop exploring the Next.

It's not enough to deal with changes as they come along. You also need to stay on top of the trends that are transforming your industry, the economy and the world. Never stop looking out for the latest challenge or opportunity: a new tool, technology or customer wish.

Change resilience is about the excitement of the exploration. When you know your cause, it's easy to understand which opportunities to pursue. You want to achieve results, so you relent-lessly seek new, better, faster ways to fulfil your promise. Not only are you no longer reluctant to embrace change, you thrive on it.

2. Stop living in fear.

We're all going to experience some bad situations – that's life. Per-haps we'll deal with a customer who exploits a loophole to his or her advantage. Maybe a rogue employee will take advantage of the company's generous vacation policy. Maybe we'll have a bad experi-ence with a new technology.

The main difference between those with change resilience and those without it is how we respond to such situations.

Our natural reaction may be to prevent anything like that from happening again. We therefore establish restrictive policies that limit what customers and employees can do. Or we close ourselves off to new opportunities.

By doing so, we treat everyone as a potential abuser unless proven otherwise. Unfortunately, such restrictive processes and rigid rules have a way of eroding trust. In the name of thwarting a few abusers, we treat everyone suspiciously and destroy our chance at strengthening our change resilience.

I've always found this tendency fascinating, but not in a good way. All it takes is one bad apple for many of us to decide that all apples must be bad. How does that make sense?

Yet we do it every day. On the organizational level, the bean counters and the legal eagles are focused on minimizing and mit-igating risk. They do so by creating overgeneralized rules –

'just to be safe' – that affect millions of customers and create pain for thousands of employees. Such rules make it more difficult to work with the organization. They make it difficult for the organization to change.

On a personal level, we limit our ability to meet new people, learn new things and see new places.

What's the alternative? Recognizing that just because one person acted badly, we do not need to punish everyone. We cannot live life beset by a constant fear of evil. We must put our trust in people if we are to adapt and evolve. We can learn from our experiences with those who took advantage of us – and trust that those experiences were the exceptions, not the rule.

3. Keep it simple and flexible.

Can you live by the rule "Always do the right thing for all parties involved"? It's a simple rule, but it asks people to do what they think is best for the customer, their organization and themselves.

I am sure that such a rule frightens some chief legal and compliance officers. They cannot envision such simplicity. So let me pose the question differently: Have you read your company's compliance policies? If you're a manager, how many of your employees know and fully understand the five-inch-thick rule book they're given when they're hired? How many people remember any of those rules five minutes after their training ends?

Let's face it: these rule books are 'gotcha' tools. They are there to prove to the employee, in the case of a mistake, that he or she has failed. They are not really guiding anyone and they're certainly not building trust. If anything, they eliminate trust and turn employees into compliance robots who refuse to think for themselves.

Living with change resilience is about creating simple trust-based guidelines and keeping our options and opportunities open. It's about refusing to allow bad experiences to close us off to new experiences.

More importantly, change resilience is about drawing strength from our successes, living by the impact we have created, and increasing our change resilience in the process. For every bad experience we have with a customer, we have had several that were inspiring, exciting, rewarding. Why should we allow the bad experiences to define who we are and determine which opportunities we explore in the future?

4. Let your core cause guide you.

It seemed like a fun task – at first. During a consulting project, I'd been assigned to help the reception team during the check-in process at a family resort. The resort had changed hands twice during the past four years and was struggling to establish itself as a provider of great customer experiences. By around 1pm, the lobby was full of families who'd just driven three hours and were now ready to embark on different types of activities. The only obstacle between them and their long-anticipated vacation was reception – and, as you can imagine, there was impatience in the air.

While the young staff members were checking in the guests, I handed out welcome kits and chatted with the families. I almost immediately noticed that one of the teenage boys in a family of four was in a bad mood. I tried to get him to smile, and his mom said, "Good luck with that."

I could see in her eyes the helplessness of the parent of a teenager – the same feeling I experienced when my kids were that age. You want to make them happy, but you simply don't know how. The old tricks do not work anymore. Coming to this resort was her idea of getting the family together in a fun environment. She was hoping that maybe a few smiles might appear on her son's face.

The employee completing the check-in process was efficient – collecting credit cards and confirming reservations at lightning speed. She had probably issued more room keys than anyone else at the desk. In fact, she was so efficient that she hardly got a chance to look those guests in the eye. She was what I refer to as a 'process performer' through and through.

Meanwhile, I eventually achieved my goal. The teenager smiled. Maybe not for a *long* time – he was definitely doing me a favour by moving his facial muscles, however temporarily. But, hey, you need to set your expectations accordingly when it comes to teenagers. More importantly, I could see his mother was happy.

As I celebrated this small victory, the front-desk employee was completely oblivious to the human drama playing out a few feet away. She was already preparing to process the next family. It was at that moment that I recognized how dangerous it is to be a process performer. It wasn't this employee's fault that she couldn't connect with this family – as a young single person, she had no clue what it meant to be a parent. She could not relate – let alone understand how her core cause connected to serving this family. As a result, she was treating the check-in process as an end goal and not merely as a vehicle to give families a chance to bond and enter into a great vacation experience.

She'd never learned how to connect her core cause to her performance.

As you pursue new and exciting ways to deliver value and connect with people, let your core cause be your guide. Remember, your core cause is what got you here. You are not here randomly, but rather are driven by purpose.

Your core cause is a unique prism through which to evaluate new opportunities to change and evolve. As a tried-and-true intrinsic compass, your core cause will serve several purposes:

1. **Guide:** Your core cause will help you understand which new opportunities to explore and which ones to abandon. It will show you how the next transformation will help you fulfil your greater purpose.

2. **Inspire:** We cannot maintain a high energy level at all times. We often have down moments when we need inspiration. In those moments, let your core cause remind you of the beauty of your purpose and the people who need you. Think about your vision of a better world – the world you are attempting to create.

3. **Refuel:** Allow your past successes in serving your core cause to act as a reminder that you can work through whatever today's hardship is and emerge triumphant. If you're part of a team, allow your collective memories to lift you up and overcome the challenging moments.

4. **Support:** Always review the lessons you've learned in pursuit of your core cause – even those you consider failures. Think of them as swings that didn't result in home runs but that served as important practice.

5. Remember that change can be liberating.

When Pampers introduced disposable diapers in 1961, the reaction was lukewarm to negative. The product was perceived as distorting the image of the ideal mother: real mothers took care of their children in many ways, one of which was by washing their dirty cloth diapers. This negative reaction slowed the adoption of disposable diapers in the marketplace considerably.

Those who initially opposed Pampers were making a simple mistake. They defined a good mother as a doer of domestic chores, not as a nurturer and educator. It was only when the perception of the mother's role evolved that people could see how the product liberated them to be better caregivers. Mothers could now focus on nurturing their kids and loving them, rather than toiling at the wash buckets and cleaning up dirty diapers. Children benefited far more from high-quality time with their mothers and extra bedtime stories than they did from their mothers cleaning cloth diapers.

When motherhood was defined in the context of its impact on children, change was much more easily absorbed; as a result, millions of mothers were transformed from human washing machines to nurturing, loving caregivers.

We all have the opportunity to start viewing change as a liberation. Just as a new product can liberate us to rethink societal roles and expectations, new systems can liberate us to take our performance to a totally new level and new technologies can free us up to focus on the human aspect of our work and add a personal and authentic touch to everything we do. After all, no two smiles look exactly the same – and yet, if they are authentic, they'll all generate tremendous emotional engagement.

Loving Change Resilience

So, how do you know if you're change resilient?

Well, we all love to complete a challenge. Hit a milestone. Cross a finish line.

Unfortunately, change resilience isn't a goal. It's a way of being in the world.

There is, however, one way you can tell you're on the right track. It will happen when you start looking forward to change. When you embrace change resilience as a mission and not a mandate. When change feels like a desire, not a chore. When we start loving the changed person we have become, we know we have arrived. But we won't stop there. With our eyes always scanning the horizon for the Next, we will continue the transformation.

A world in which people stop changing is a world without progress. Our job as human beings is not to just accept the world the way it is, but to build it as we want it to be.

I hope you're as excited about the Next as I am.

with gratitude

Writing this book is first and foremost an act of trust. During the past 15 years, our clients and their employees have trusted me and Strativity with their transformations and strategic changes. There were many dark moments of fear and anxiety before we saw the light. My first gratitude is extended to all those clients and their employees. They opened their hearts and, in the process, opened my eyes to their challenges – allowing me to be their Sherpa on the journey to a better future.

My next gratitude extends to the Strativity team, who worked with me closely to execute on over 200 transformation projects. Your passion and dedication, your commitment and creativity enabled us to inspire more than one million employees so far to overcome their fear of change and turn change into a natural evolution that inspires their future. To Michael B., Jason, Joe, Ed, Tim, Lacey, Danny, Ali, Michelle, Kelly, Wayne, Ari, Peter, Guido, Ildi, Anthony, Steve, Bree, Edward, Marcus, Ben, Shanel, Brad, Cyrus, George, AJ, Alexis, Ezio, Frank, Monica, Marwan, Rocco, Steven W. Tyler, Andrew and the Australia team, as well as our amazing executive facilitators, who are too numerous to mention.

Trusting a new manuscript and guiding it through publication is a fascinating and careful process. I would like to extend

243

my deepest gratitude to my agent, Leila Campoli, for her tireless dedication and endless enthusiasm supporting the book. To Michelle Martin for believing in the book. To Jess, who worked with me on developing my manuscript. To the team at LID Publishing for the UK edition of this book, Sara, Caroline, Maria and Martin. I thought I knew how to write, but you really took that writing to the next level.

My last and deepest expression of gratitude goes to my dear family. My parents, my dear wife, Drora, and my five wonderful children, Dalya, Cheli, Liad, Netanel and Ronya. This book is my gift to you. May you learn to soar with change and inspire your future.